The Home We Shared

History and Memoir of the
North Dakota Children's Home at
Fargo, North Dakota

Dorothy A. Lund Nelson

Photos by
Amil J. Lund

Text copyright © 2004 by Dorothy Alberna Lund Nelson

Photos copyright © 2004 by Dorothy A. Lund Nelson for her late father, Amil J. Lund, and The Village Family Service Center, Fargo, North Dakota

Edited by Tammy Noteboom
Cover design and book layout by Laurie E. Neill

All rights reserved. No part of this book or photos may be reproduced or transmitted in any form or by any means, electronic or mechanical, including: photocopying, recording, or by any information storage and retrieval system, without permission in writing from the publisher.

Contact:

Lectures on Leisure by Lund
Attention: Dorothy A. Lund Nelson
2910 – 22nd Street South East
Rochester, MN 55904
Phone or Fax: 507-282-6269
E-mail: dlundnelson@hotmail.com

First Edition – Printed April, 1991, in the U.S.A. by
PAPER AND GRAPHICS, Rochester, MN 55906

Second Edition (Revised) — Printed September, 2004 in the U.S.A. by

Davies Printing Company
2715 Pennington Ct. NW
Rochester, MN 55901

Library of Congress Cataloging-in-Publication Date-Lund Nelson, Dorothy A., 1933-
"The Home We Shared" written by Dorothy A. Lund Nelson
Photos by Amil J. Lund
and Photo File of The Village Family Service Center

ISBN 0-9701277-1-5

Autobiography; 1-Children's Home; 2-Orphanage; 3-Child Care, Positive;
4-Orphans; 5-Adoptions; 6-Camping Experiences;
7-North Dakota History

Summary: A historical account of life in the North Dakota Children's Home in Fargo, North Dakota, through the memoir of the houseparent's daughter, Dorothy. The reasons the children were placed in the Children's Home and their daily experiences.

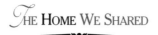
The Home We Shared

In Memory of

My parents,
Amil Justin Lund and Mary Alberna Leazer Lund
and sister, Myra Dean Lund Schlosser

To Honor

All of the Children who once lived at the
North Dakota Children's Home
and
The Children's Home Staff,
who gave many hours of service to the children.

Dedicated to

My sons,
Norman and wife, Mia;
Scott and wife, Sharon;
and Weston.

My grandchildren,
Sarah, Nicole, and Jasmine.

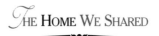

The Children's Prayer

This was prayed in unison
by the children at the
North Dakota Children's Home
before each meal.

Bless us Father 'ere we eat,
Keep us healthy, wise and sweet,
Make us loving, kind, and good,
So we may serve You as we should.
Amen.

CONTENTS

Introduction, 2004	1
Preface, 1991	2
Forward, 1991	3
Our Home	5
The North Dakota Children's Home	7
Reasons Children Arrived at the Home	9
Poverty	10
The "Different" Child	15
The Unplanned Pregnancy	18
Neglect and Abuse	30
Crippled Children's Program and Summer Program for the Children's Home Resident Children	35
History of the Home	43
Andrew Horace Burke	44
Frank Drew Hall	49
Fundraisers	58
Laura Rundle	62
Dr. C.J. Dillon	65
Lucy J. (Babcock) Hall	68
Harold H. Bond	72
Robert C. Olslund	83
Mabel Miller	85
Remembering Some of the Other Workers	87
Our Shared Parents	93
Mary Albearna Leazer Lund	94
Amil Justine Lund	98
Mary and Amil	100
Our Shared Home — Dorothy's A. Lund Nelson's Memoir	107
Fall Season (Age Birth to Five) 1933-1938	108
Winter Season (Age Six to 10) 1939-1943	112
Spring Season (Ages 11-15) 1944-1948	121
Summer Season (Ages 16 to 22) 1949-1955	131
Other Children Share Their Memories of Our Home	147
Hazel Baringer Hoeppner	148
May Berge Bredeson	153
Margaret Wogh	155
Florence Wiest Faust	158
Alton Graf	163
Rosalie Reis Rosenaw	166
Royal Wayne Bahr	169
Dorothy Noell Anderson	175
Delbert Knowlen	177
Gloria Wang	179
Alice Tannehill	182
Siblings Reunited After 48 Years	184
Meta Mae Madden	185
A Walking Tour	187
Remarks by Mr. Lund, November 14, 1963	200
Acknowledgements	203

The Home We Shared

Introduction, 2004

Recently, three happenings awakened my desire to re-write my book, "Orphan Home, 'Orphan'," concerning the North Dakota Children's Home where I had the privilege of living for 22 years.

The first happening occurred while sharing my presentation, "Orphan Train Riders" with the staff of "The Village Family Service Center." At four different locations, I presented stories of the New York City children who were "placed out" with many families across America during the years of 1854-1929.

I closed the program with historical facts and a slide presentation about the North Dakota Children's Home from 1928-1955. The Village team took great interest in this history, as The Village is the current name for the original Children's Home Society.

During the presentation of these programs for The Village, many memories returned and I was at "The Home We Shared."

The second happening that reawakened my desire to write my story was reading two books written by people who received cruel and unloving experiences while wards of the Minnesota State School at Owattona, Minnesota. These types of experiences were foreign to me and it was most difficult for me to read about the horrendous treatment some of those children received.

Like most things in this world, one cannot label orphanages "all bad" or "all good;" there must have been life "in-between," as well. But, I feel that most experiences at the North Dakota Children's Home were positive.

The third happening came during the rewrite in the form of a phone call from a special woman who sought information about the Home. She had recently uncovered the fact she lived at the Home the first 14 months of her life. Her questions flowed, "Where was it located? Who took care of me? What did I wear? Where did I sleep? What did I eat?"

Because of the difference in our ages, I knew that most likely, I had dressed, rocked, and fed her. If not I, certainly my mother, Mary, would have been responsible for her care.

Through her inquiring, I realized that many persons would desire this information, also. Possibly, other persons who were too young to remember the experience, but know that they were raised at the Home. I was ready to share the history of this special place.

These three events inspired the desire within me to rewrite and publish this book in a more acceptable manner. (It was originally typed on a small PC and 100 books printed on a copy machine.)

I felt the need to retell the history of daily life in the Home and preserve the facilities history.

Now, please come with me, as we go to "The Home We Shared."

- Dorothy A. Lund Nelson, 2004

The Home We Shared

Preface, 1991

Until just recently, history has been a compilation of wars, dates, famous men and events. The span of history, Pericles, marking the beginning and Haley, (now) marking the end, was consumed with stories of the most powerful, with the writer being in direct hire by the person wishing to be immortalized; the man with the budget.

In the 1960s, a new movement entered history departments throughout the United States; the movement held that the lives of the poor, underclass individuals contained a historical record valuable beyond their utility merely as statistics.

Students, who studied Washington's life from the chopped down cherry tree to the crossing of the Delaware, now read of his "owner of slaves" lifestyle.

Alex Haley's, "Roots," popularized the historical method of collecting oral history as history, valid because it represented life as it was experienced. Since then, historians have been researching, collecting and teaching more than dates and empty facts. Now, they can never return to a history conveniently devoid of "little people."

Dorothy Lund's book adds to the historical record of the orphans of the Children's Home. The statistics of the Depression years "speak for themselves;" of the hardships people endured. They don't speak as loudly, however, as the orphan children, who cry out to be remembered.

Like Doctor Seuss,' "Horton Hears the Who," wherein Horton put his ear to the dust speck and heard the people in Whosville shout "We're here!" Dorothy Lund has interviewed persons, collected photos, and recalled her life to announce the "Little People Are Here!" Now they will not be forgotten as long as we strain to listen.

Weston J.Barnhart Lund, — 1991
BA, Hamline University, St.Paul, Minnesota; RPCV-Morocco;
MA, Teachers College Columbia University, New York City, New York

The Home We Shared

Forward to "Orphan Home, 'Orphan'" -1991
The North Dakota Children's Home
My Home for 22 Years!

A few years ago, a serious accident caused me to be encircled in a body cast for seven months. While I was lying flat on my back, I began to write many memories into a notebook. I wrote about feelings, events, and experiences of my years as a youngster.

This reminiscence therapy, as it is called, brought to me the comforting care which my mother, Mary Leazer Lund, and my father, Amil J. Lund, gave so frequently to others and myself. I discovered there were a wealth of experiences to be recalled.

As I reviewed my years at the North Dakota Children's Home, I challenged my dad, Amil, to draw a floor plan of the facility and I drew mine. When we compared our drawings, we discovered we both remembered the Home in great detail, which brought out more stories from both Dad and I.

Being the only child that never left the Home over a period of 22 years, I **REMEMBERED**:

— **the excitement of many Christmas parties.** Before Christmas, the Children's Home Staff selected gifts for every child, usually clothing and a few toys. Churches, service clubs, and friends throughout the state donated these presents or gifts of money.

— **the clanging sound of the school bell.** Ten minutes before meals, a worker rang the bell, giving each child enough time to get in from the playground and wash up. When the bell rang a second time, we all rushed to the dining room.

— **the squeals from children in the playroom.** When I was a toddler, my parents brought me to the playroom to play with the other children. Then as a youth, I took my turn at entertaining or baby sitting the children in the playroom. A little slide stood in the center. From a closet, we could pull mats for tumbling and other play equipment.

— **the good smells of the fresh bread, elephant ears, and cookies donated by the Dutch Maid Bakery.** The children enjoyed these immensely! As for myself, the numerous servings of bread pudding, produced from the extra loaves of bread, were NOT a treat. To this day, I cannot understand why anyone would pay for bread pudding at a restaurant!

— **the wonderful summers spent at Lake Pelican at Camp Watson.** At Camp Watson, we swam three to four times a day, wore small amounts of clothing, and received great tans. We ate most meals outdoors, unless the weather was not cooperating. The boys built stilts and conducted contests; the girls played house with their dolls and play furniture. We watched colorful sunsets, weathered out many severe storms, and awoke to bright morning sunrises.

The Home We Shared

— **the yells of "Ante-I-Over"** as the ball left the opponent's hands and our team rushed to catch it. Night after night, we played the game over the double garage behind the Home.

— **the boys being taken for their monthly haircuts.** The Barber College could take 10 boys at a time, which filled all the chairs at the school. The barber students gave the best FREE haircuts!

— **the horizontal lines of the girls' bobbed hair.** I think my mother was the barber for the girls. The style was straight bangs with the rest cut below the ears and around to the back of the neck. I know I was the only female child with long hair. My apologies to the other girls!

— **the WORK we shared.** In any large family there has to be organization, sharing, and order. Thus, as we reached the age of 10 or 12, we were required to take on some responsibilities; setting or clearing tables, washing dishes, folding clothes, making beds, sweeping floors, or watching over younger children. Work, at least to me, seemed almost like play, as it was usually done in a group. There was always someone to talk to and work beside.

— **the arrival of children.** This is when we all had some unhappy thoughts of living in the Home. Realizing these children had to leave their parents. Knowing how much they wanted to be with their parents and that it may never be possible. Learning that many siblings would be adopted separately. Hearing stories about children turned down by adoptive parents because of hair or skin color.

— **the children leaving.** When someone left the Home, it meant they were being separated not only from their brothers and sisters; but, also, from their playmates, their swimming companions, their work partners, and dormitory mates. For me, it was a constant time of "goodbyes." I must have said my farewells to thousands of babies and children.

Thinking back on my life at the Home, I have positive feelings. I hope this is true for others who lived there too! But knowing the various reasons for their arrival, each child's attitude and perspective would be different than mine. I do feel the children received well-rounded care. Health was a concern, food was good, education was encouraged, and love was shown even through discipline.

The 100th Year Celebration Picnic on July 22, 1991, should give all of us a good time to reflect on our childhood days. Let's hope that we can do some positive therapeutic reminiscing!

Dorothy Lund, 1991

P.S. My father, Amil, attended the 1991 picnic. It was his last visit to Fargo. He enjoyed meeting all of his Home children. We returned to Rochester, Minnesota, to my home, where he lived his last year. He died on October 31, 1991.

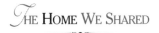

OUR HOME
AT 804 10TH STREET SOUTH
FARGO, NORTH DAKOTA

1900-1957

The Home We Shared

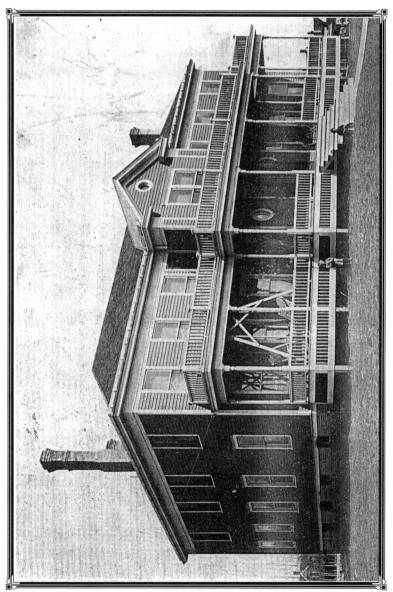

Early photo of North Dakota Children's Home. The left-hand portion of this building was erected in 1900; the south wing and porches were added later. This building was used until 1957 when the Children's Village was occupied.

The Home We Shared

The North Dakota Children's Home

From 1900 to 1957, a huge wooden mansion stood on the corner of 10th Street and 8th Avenue South in Fargo, North Dakota. It was a massive building compared to the one-family homes on the block. A large lawn, a fully equipped playground, and a ball field completed the half block surrounding the awesome structure.

The front of the Home faced 10th Street and had a porch on both its first and second floors. These two long porches were gated with evenly spaced wooden spindles holding up the railings, making the Home look like a double-decker sandwich.

The second floor porch had three doors, two leading to girls' bedrooms and one to a toddlers' nursery. A metal fire escape descended off the south end of the porch. The Children's Home Staff often used the second floor porch for "sunning" babies and toddlers in their wicker bassinets, plaid buggies, built in "cubbies," or white metal cribs.

Midway, on the lower porch, was the wide front door that opened out onto two tiers of stairs: the first of wood and the second of cement. All flowed out onto a wide sidewalk with a curved lip that met the main sidewalk and street like a gray-white carpet. It offered a welcoming view to all new arrivals to the Home.

Steps into the Home, 1930.

New friends.

The Home We Shared

Over a span of 57 years, this entrance welcomed over 9,000 children. Small children were carried by their parents, social workers or relatives across the "carpet," up the stairs, and through the heavy door. Older children would cling to their escorts as they approached the building.

Giggling girls, circa 1920.

Resting on our front porch, circa 1920.

Parents relinquished their children to "The Home," hoping adoption would give them a better life; a style of life they were not able to provide at that time. Birth parents firmly believed that adopting couples would give loving care to their children.

While children awaited adoption, the staff of the Children's Home supplied personal care, love, clothing, food and cleanliness. Local doctors watched over their medical care, as well.

Eventually, these children would have another place to call "home," as the movement of children and adult caretakers flowed outward as well. Thousands of children were adopted, "placed out" into foster care, or returned to their parents when the parents were able to care for them.

The adopting parents, foster parents, and social workers led children out from Children's Home toward homes with smaller, more permanent families. "To find a good home for each child" was the ultimate goal.

The Home We Shared

Reasons Children Arrived at the Home

Poverty
The Different Child
The Unplanned Pregnancy
Neglect and Abuse
the Crippled Children's Program

The Home We Shared

Arriving at the Home

A variety of situations brought children to the North Dakota Children's Home. Through the following fictitious stories, I hope to share some of the pain and grief the parents and their children might have felt. Many difficult circumstances resulted in the final decisions of separation. The realization that their children would have better surroundings made it seem right.
Let us imagine....

Poverty

It was October of 1937. The trees were beginning to show their annual display of colors, bright hues of reddish-orange with only the faintest hint of the ever-persistent green.

Julia arose early, which was her custom, in order to enjoy her morning solitude. It was her time of quiet before the bustle of making breakfast and preparing the children for school. She walked through the rambling old farmhouse to the back door. As she pushed open the screen door, the spring gave a soft stretching sound. Julia looked out and witnessed the sky aglow from the sun sliding gently over the horizon. Soon, the sun revealed faint graying paint on the wood barn.

Nearby, the few unbroken windows of the chicken coop reflected the red-yellow of the morning light. The "cock-a-doodle-do," of a lone rooster brought a smile to her face. She walked on past the building towards the fields. "This is the best time of the day," thought Julia, as she stepped over the large cracks in the hardened earth.

Her thoughts returned to the mid-twenties, "Oh, how Albert and I enjoyed the farm."

In her mind, she pictured the 1925 farm. The barnyard swarmed with animals — cows, pigs, and sheep. The shadows of their tractor, rake, and hay wagon cast upon the white painted barn.

Then, she recalled the sight of Bill calling out, "Daddy, may I help?" as he trotted behind his dad.

"Me help, too?" came the little voice of Amy toddling as fast as she could behind her brother.

Julia's mind swept quickly to the Depression and the birth of the twins, Jane and Jean, in 1929. "Albert was such a dependable guy!" she thought, "He always found a way to work things out so we had good food on our table; though sometimes, just barely enough."

She remembered how potatoes became the main course of food. First digging them from her small garden. Then, scrubbing off the dirt. Finally, preparing them in various ways to appear on the dining room table: french fries, baked, lefse, twice baked, mashed, boiled with onions, or American fries. Other vegetables took their turns on the table in a variety of forms, too. All these memories made her chuckle. The family never complained about her new creations from the kitchen.

The Home We Shared

"Thank goodness for popcorn! It was the most exciting food for the family! How often I served it for a meal." She continued her thoughts, "It really was the last resort, but the children thought the Popcorn Meal was a 'party.' They did not realize it was our most meager meal."

Wayne and Helen were born in the early '30s. Shortly after their births, Albert contracted "the consumption" or tuberculosis, and died. The years since his death had been hard on all of them.

"Albert, bless his soul," Julia whispered, "Oh, Lord, it has become so very difficult without him."

After Albert's death, there was less to divide among the seven of them. Julia sold the land one-acre at a time for very low prices. Now, she only owned a two-acre garden, the barnyard, and the land around the house. Because of the drought, the garden produced very little this year.

"Only enough land to give us our daily bread," Julia spoke as in offering a soft prayer. "How do I make ends meet?" she said lifting her head towards the sky.

Grasping her apron, she pulled it upwards and buried her face into it. "What will happen to the children?" she sighed, "Perhaps Reverend Swenson was right. It might be time for me to consider the Children's Home in Fargo."

The words of her pastor came to mind. "Julia, at the Home your children will be clothed properly, fed good meals, and attend school regularly. Doctors will take care of any health problems and the children will have a warm clean house to live in. Possibly, you could find work and increase your income." He continued, "Then, in a few years, you might settle in a new place or return to the farm. At that time, the children could return to you."

Julia thought out loud, "Today, I must speak to Bill and Amy about their future. For a sixteen-year-old, Bill is such a young man. While Amy, our beautiful fourteen-year-old has become a second mother to all of the brood." The thoughts of her two older youth made Julia feel so happy, as she had such great pride in them.

"Mother," came the words of a young girl, "I heard you talking. Is someone here?"

"Yes," Julia spoke hesitantly. "I was talking to the Lord. He seems to have put a special glow on the horizon this morning." She rambled on nervously, "This warm glow has given me the courage to discuss an important problem with you and Bill. Please wake him up."

Moments later, Bill arrived at the back door with Amy. Together, the two slid quietly through the screen door. They were careful not to allow the spring to snap it shut. They realized that their mother did not want the other children to be awakened.

The teenagers walked towards their mother and each slid an arm under one of her arms. The three walked into the morning sunlight. Julia extended her arms around their waists in a family embrace.

"Bill and Amy, I am trying to make a big decision! It will affect all of you children. It is something I can hardly bare to think about." Julia hesitated, then, with a new breath continued to speak, "It hurts me so deeply, but I have to decide quickly before winter roars in on us."

Bill and Amy watched their mother's face and realized that she was about to cry. They could only remember her crying once; that was at their father's funeral.

"What is troubling you, Mom?" asked Bill.

"Did we do something wrong?" Amy inquired, as she drew her mother in close.

"Oh, no, children," Julia continued with new strength in her voice, "You know that Reverend Swenson has stopped here frequently the past two months. He's been trying to help me understand that I must make a plan for raising all of you children."

"Oh, Mom, I didn't realize that things were that bad," Bill said in surprise.

"Bill, there is no more money. I have no more land to sell. The garden did not produce much for us this year. Each day we have less and less food to eat. There is no way to keep our home warm as I cannot afford coal and all the wood is gone. This winter could be a very difficult one for all of us! Possibly, one of us might not even survive until spring."

Amy looked at Bill wondering what her mother and the pastor had come up with for a solution, "What are you thinking about doing?" asked the worried teenager.

"Well, Reverend Swenson has suggested that the six of you might go to Fargo and live in the North Dakota Children's Home. I would hope that I could find a job and in two or more years, earn enough money to find a place to live in Minot or Dickinson." Julia ended her dream statements in a firm voice, "Then, we could all move back together again!"

Bill and Amy were shocked. They could not imagine their mother giving them up to strangers.

"How could you be thinking about such a thing?" Bill said sharply.

Amy began to cry as she ran towards the house, "I DON'T want to GO to ANY CHILDREN'S HOME!" Then, even more loudly she yelled, "DON'T DO THIS TO US, MOM!"

Bill put his arms around Julia's shoulders and together they walked to the house, "Mom, I don't want to go either; but, I realize that you and pastor have talked this over and thought it through." He hesitated and said, "You know what is best for all of us. How soon do you think this will happen?"

"The sooner the better, Bill." Julia returned his hug saying, "Thanks for being supportive." She added, "We all have to believe that this is for the better."

All of the children were summoned to the kitchen and Julia explained, "Within two weeks you will be traveling by car to Fargo with Reverend

The Home We Shared

Swanson. He will take you to a children's home. You will take a few clothes and toys. I will write to you regularly. Remember, I'll always be your mother and will miss you very much!"

Just as planned, the children were packed and ready when the pastor drove into the farmyard. Julia gave a long, intense embrace to each child with a promise to be joined as a family within two years. She had decided to say her good-byes at the farm rather than ride the five hours to Fargo and give these difficult farewells at the Home.

Two years passed and Julia's dream did not come true. The jobs she found hardly paid for her own expenses. She realized she would have to place her children for adoption. She learned that Bill and Amy were too old for adoption. They were encouraged to finish school at Fargo Central High School. After graduation, the staff at the Home would assist them in finding employment and places to live.

The other children — Jane, Jean, Wayne, and Helen would be adopted. Julia signed the necessary papers so the social workers could begin the process of finding families and homes for them.

The twins would be adopted together; but there was no guarantee the other two younger children would be placed in the same home.

Julia traveled to Fargo to say one final "Goodbye" to her children. She spent some hours with Bill and Amy. She praised them for their accomplishments and the three made plans to visit regularly in the future.

While visiting with the younger four in the library at the Home, she felt they were distant from her. They chatted about their new friends, school, and meals. She realized they were well settled into a special life at the Home.

The loss of these children was a most traumatic and sorrowful time for Julia. She likened it to six deaths, actually, seven deaths when she included the death of Albert, her husband, just a few years prior.

A 1930's family.

THE HOME WE SHARED

Factual Comments:

After each war and during the Depression years, there was an influx of children in family units to the Home. This would have been related to a loss of a parent in a war and/or poverty. These groups of children sometimes arrived undernourished, in ragged clothing, and dirty. Many children arrived alone.

The workers immediately took the children to the large upstairs bathroom and began the process of cleaning them up. They cut and deloused their hair. Then, they gave each child a soapy bath. The children had to walk up a set of wooden steps to get into the large tub. It was elevated so a caretaker could stand beside it and scrub the children. Next, they were dressed in clean clothes and fed a nourishing meal. Then, they would be introduced to the other children and staff. Finally, each was given a guided tour through the building to help them understand where they would be living.

A family photo, 1928.

Since children arrived anytime, day or night, the workers went through this procedure frequently. It was the workers first actions to show the children they cared about them.

The "Different" Child

Excitement reigned at Alice and Raymond's home. They were expecting their third child. They had two darling daughters, Katie and Andrea, and were now hoping for a boy. All predictions pointed to the fact that this child might fulfill their dream.

One prediction came from her friends, "Alice, you are carrying this child much lower, so it will definitely be a boy."

The other came from the family doctor after he listened to the baby's heartbeat, "Your baby seems to have a faster heartbeat," he said, "It could be a boy; I know how much you have wanted a son."

"Oh, yes, especially Raymond wishes for a son to carry on his carpentry trade; a son for a hunting and fishing buddy." Alice said, "Oh, yes, and a son to continue on the family name."

The day came for Alice to give birth. The child arrived very quickly. Much to the delight of both parents, the baby WAS A BOY! The excitement of the birth of a male child carried through the complete family and their circle of friends. They named the child, "Charles," after Raymond's father.

While bathing her baby, Alice would look into his blue eyes and he would respond with a big smile; the smile was his trademark! He seemed to be a happy child.

However, as the months went by, Alice became concerned, as Charlie was not responding in his motor skills the same way as their daughters had at the same age; nor, was he making any baby sounds. At the age of six months, he could not roll over or even attempt to sit upright when held in that position. Alice would get on the floor with him and try to help him learn to crawl.

When he reached his first birthday, he could move a little bit on the floor; when he was two years old, he began to sit up and could balance on his feet for a few seconds.

Raymond would hold his son and say, "You are such a good child. Oh, how I wish you could walk! You are a blessing to our household with your smiles. I love you so much."

Placing a kiss on the child's forehead, Raymond would lower Charlie into his crib. Then, he would tousle the child's ringlets as he slid his fingers through Charlie's bright, red hair.

Raymond tried not to show his disappointment to the family; but often in the solitude of his workshop, tears would come to his eyes as he reflected on his son. He knew this child would not be able to meet the expectations of his dreams.

As the next three years went by, Alice and Raymond realized they had a "different" child. Charlie continued to be slower compared to the children of their friends. He now could walk, but not run with the other children. He could say a few words, but not make sentences. They decided to consult with their family doctor, as Charlie was nearing school age.

"Doctor Olson, we need some help. We all know that our child is not normal; but, what are we to do?" Raymond asked.

"You have a happy-go-lucky child with a brilliant smile. He has brought joy to your home; but now you need to think of his future," replied the doctor. "It is time to take special tests to decide whether or not he can attend school. You can have those tests done through the school system."

The parents followed the doctor's directions and after the tests were completed the report came back saying, "Charles is not educable."

They consulted the doctor again. "If Charlie cannot learn, what do you suggest we do, now?" Alice inquired.

"You could consider placing him in the State School and Hospital at Grafton, North Dakota. It is a place for children and adults, who are physically or mentally handicapped and unable to take care of themselves," Dr. Olson said.

Thus, the doctor assisted them in filling out the forms for a "hearing of committal" and for entrance into the state hospital.

Everything went well with the hearing and placement, except word came to the parents that the institution had no openings for new residents at that time.

"Doctor, now what happens?" asked Alice.

"There is a place called the North Dakota Children's Home in Fargo. This place will care for your child until he can be received into the state hospital. I will make the contacts for you."

It was an extremely painful day for the family, when the social worker arrived to transport Charles to his new Home. The sisters and parents hugged him and cried.

"Oh, Charlie, we will miss you so much," each chimed in. "We hate to have you leave us."

Factual Comments:

Frequently, "different" children arrived at the Home. There, the nurses and community doctors cared for them until they could be admitted to the state hospital.

While at the Home, the workers would tend to their physical and mental needs. My mother, Mary, firmly believed and would tell me, "The more this child can do and achieve before entering Grafton hospital, the easier it will be for the child when he or she is finally admitted."

She worked with the staff to help them understand how to improve the child's physical condition. Thus, all of the workers assisted the child in the same manner. Often, the workers at the Home wished these children would not have to be institutionalized at Grafton; but court orders had to be followed.

In one instance, a dear 10-year-old boy spent at least one year at the

The Home We Shared

Home. During the summer, he was able to be at Camp Watson. My parents did not want him to go to Grafton, but they had no say in his destiny.

About 30 years later, because of new laws established for the care of Mentally and Physically Challenged, this young man was released from the Grafton Institution. He, like many institution residents, was placed in a North Dakota community.

When my father, Amil, was in his 80s, he was walking on a Fargo street when the same young man stopped him and said, "Hello, Mr. Lund." He introduced himself. My father was amazed that in all those years the fellow still remembered him. Dad learned he was living in a group home and had a job at a thrift shop. How good it was to discover the young man could live and work in Fargo.

THE HOME WE SHARED

THE UNPLANNED PREGNANCY

Harriet was a senior at Edgeley High School. It was springtime, just a few months before her graduation. But, this spring, Harriet was not very happy. She awoke each morning with a queasy stomach. As she dressed in her small bedroom in the family's one-and-a-half-story home, she could not focus on her school day.

She walked down the steps to the kitchen. Her mom greeted her, "Harriet, you look rather pale today. I notice you are not as energetic as you used to be. Is something wrong?"

"No, Mom, I just didn't sleep well last night. I'll be OK after I have eaten," she replied, knowing full well that the food would not stay with her for long. She most certainly would become nauseous very shortly and hurry to the toilet to heave the food out. After cleaning herself up, she gave her mom a hug, "I'll be home about 4:30, Mom."

She left the frame house and walked up Main Street towards the high school. As she approached her school, she met one of her classmates, "What are you going to wear to the prom, Harriet?"

"Oh, Jane, I don't even think I will go. With Dave off to war, I feel I should just stay home." She continued, "It just doesn't seem right for me to be out partying when he is sitting in a foxhole."

"Well, you are always welcome to join us at a table and dance a few numbers with Jim."

The girls hurried into the school and prepared for their classes. Near the lockers, there was more discussion among the senior girls about the prom.

Harriet thought, "I simply don't care about this event. I miss Dave so much." She turned to face the open locker so no one could see her face and tried to hold back tears, "Oh, why did he have to be called into the Army last summer? It is so scary! World War II has taken my 18-year-old-sweetheart to France. He is amid all the warring action with Germany."

Harriet took her cotton hanky and dabbed her eyes. She picked up her books for the morning classes and followed her classmates into the math room.

Amid the Algebra numbers and problems, Harriet's mind wandered to Dave's furlough in February. It was then she learned he was going overseas. They talked about marriage; however, with such short notice they decided to marry after his discharge from service.

The history class did not go much better, as Harriet daydreamed about being with Dave the last nights. Before he left Edgeley, the two spent many hours together.

"Maybe, too close," she thought, "as we had many physical experiences, which I had not felt or done before. All of our time together was most enjoyable, so loving, so exciting; but now, it is time for me to think about history."

The Home We Shared

Two weeks passed and she continued to feel much the same. "Tonight," she whispered as she got out of bed, "I will stop to see Dr. Thompson on my way home from school."

Leaving the home that morning, she told her mom and dad, "I will be later tonight. I have some things to do at school. It will be at least 5:30. See you then."

At 4 P.M., she reached the little brick office building that housed Dr. Thompson's Medical Clinic. He was a dear, old man, who had served the community for at least 25 years. He had been at her mother's side when Harriet was born.

Dr. Thompson listened carefully to Harriet's complaints. He then examined her, drew some blood for tests and said, "Please return in one week. By then, I will have the results of the tests. During this week, try to eat good food and get more sleep."

When Harriet returned the following week, Dr. Thompson looked pensive and worried. He asked Harriet to sit down next to his roll-top desk. He reached out and took her hand.

"Harriet, I have some news that is difficult to tell you," he continued as he looked over his reading glasses at her. "Harriet, you are pregnant."

"Oh, Doc, what am I going to do?"

"I presume that your special friend, David, is the father of this child. I know he cannot return to Edgeley for awhile; thus, you will have to go through this alone."

Now, Harriet became upset. She was angry and wanted to deny what her doctor was saying. She silently questioned, "How could Dave have done this to me?" Then, she remembered her own uncertainties about the last days that they had spent together, "Had she been too close and willing to 'love?' "

"Dr. Thompson, if I'm pregnant, what can I do? I know that Dave will not be able to return from France at this time," she began to cry. She was so scared. "How can I tell my mom and dad?" The questions continued, "Oh, Dr. Thompson, what will happen to my baby and me?"

Dr. Thompson placed his hand on her shoulder and said, "There are no 'ifs.' You are pregnant. I've known you all your life. I know, Harriet, that you are a very smart young lady. You will have your child and things will work out for you."

She blotted the tears from her face with her hanky and looked into his eyes. His confidence made her quiet within and she waited for him to say more.

He began slowly, "There is a place in Fargo; a place especially for young women who are in the same situation as you."

He turned to his desk, searched through the cubbyholes, and found an envelope with a return address from Fargo. He slowly opened the envelope and drew out a brochure. "I want you to read this yourself. It is about the Crittenton Home, a place for women who are expecting. You

The Home We Shared

The Florence Crittenton Home of North Dakota for Unwed Mothers.

can live there for free, as long as you assist with the making of meals and housework. They will take very good care of you and when it is time for your child to be born, you will be taken to St. John's Hospital for the birth."

Harriet was surprised she had never heard about the Crittenton Home. She was somewhat relieved by Doctor Thompson's information.

"Doctor, I have never been away from Edgeley; not even to Jamestown just a few miles away. Now, I might have to go alone all the way to Fargo. How would I get there? What do I tell others?"

"Harriet, first of all we need to tell your parents. After I close the office today, I will come to your home. You and I will break this news to your parents. Then, we can make more arrangements," the kindly man squeezed both of her hands, then assisted her to the office door. "Harriet, I know everything will work out for the good; for both you and your child."

Harriet's parents were not pleased with what they heard from their daughter and the doctor. They, too, were angry with David and that the two had been intimate.

Her mother was the first to speak, "What will the church members think of you and Dave? They always talk about girls that get themselves into 'trouble.' They are 'bad girls.' " Though she would never think of her daughter as a "bad girl," she turned to the daughter she loved and blurtted out, "You should have been able to take care of your emotions, Harriet!"

The Home We Shared

Thank goodness Doctor Thompson was present as he was able to quiet her mother by saying, "You know David and Harriet love each other very much, so now let's try to think of a good solution to this problem."

"Mom and Dad, I have some information on the Florence Crittenton Home in Fargo. It is for girls like me. Nurses and doctors will help me through the birth of the child as long as I am willing to assist with work at the facility." She handed the letter from Fargo to her parents.

Since leaving the doctor's office, Harriet had been thinking about a plan. Thus, she laid out her ideas to her parents. "I could finish the last six weeks of school and graduate. Then, I will tell my friends that I am going to Fargo to find work. In November, after the child is born I will have more decisions to make."

Her parents listened to her ideas and realized she had truly made a good plan for herself. They agreed to all she said. Doctor Thompson stated, "I am so thankful I had this information to guide you. I am proud of your ability to think this through. Now, only the four of us will know about the birth."

Soon after Harriet graduated from high school, her parents escorted her to the train station for her trip to Fargo. Many of her friends came to the station to send her on her way.

"You are so lucky to go to Fargo," said Jane. "I wish I had enough nerve to go that far from home."

The others echoed the same words. All were so impressed that Harriet was going off to work in the big city of Fargo! They were envious of her and wished they had the courage to follow her on such an adventure.

She received many hugs from her friends, but she felt the most warmth from her parents' embraces. They held her for many minutes and wished her well. "Please write often," her mother whispered in her ear, "we want to know exactly how you are doing. We love you so much!"

Then, she climbed up the steps of the passenger car and called out, "I'll see all of you at Christmas." She waved and called out once more, "See you then!"

At the Fargo Depot, a robust, well-dressed woman met Harriet at the Fargo Depot. "Are you Harriet?" she inquired as she stretched out her arm to encircle the young girl, "I am Mrs. Mattie Morgan."

Martha Morgan, head nurse at Crittenton Home, late 1920s until early 1930s.

The Home We Shared

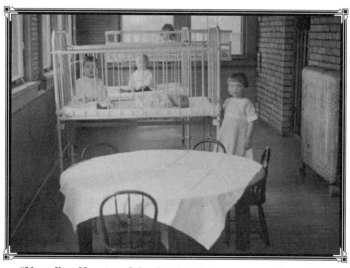

Children's nursery for mothers who chose to keep their child, Crittenton Home.

"Yes, I'm Harriet. I had talked to you on the phone, Mrs. Morgan. Thank you for meeting me, I was so nervous about arriving in Fargo."

"I am glad to meet you. You don't have to be anxious or worried now. I do hope you will enjoy your stay with us. You have many other women to meet."

The original letter stated that the head nurse at the Crittenton Home was Mrs. Morgan. Now having met her, Harriet was so relieved. "What a wonderful person," she thought. "I will not be afraid to talk to her."

They soon arrived at the brick structure. It looked as large as the Edgeley High School! "Well," she mused, "it looks like a large hotel."

As soon as she stepped inside the building, she felt comfortable. They had entered the Crittenton Home through the lower, rear level and walked through a large dining room with a huge kitchen off to the right side. Both rooms were brightly decorated.

They walked up some steps to the first floor. Mrs. Morgan showed her the large living room, offices and several classrooms. Harriet learned that the girls who had not graduated from high school would continue their schooling. Also, all would be expected to attend health classes, so they would know how to take care of themselves and their expected child, and learn about the birthing process.

On the second and third floors there were bedrooms, which two women could occupy. Mrs. Morgan took Harriet into a corner room and introduced her to her roommate. "Wanda, I would like you to meet Harriet. Harriet, this is Wanda."

"She is certainly pregnant," thought Harriet, "I wonder if I will get that big in a few months."

Harriet stepped forward and shook hands with Wanda. "I am glad that you can share your room with me."

The Home We Shared

"Oh, this isn't MY room. It is OUR room," replied Wanda. "We all understand when we arrive that we need to share a room. Judy was my roommate until she had her baby last month. Now, she has returned to her hometown."

It was late. Harriet decided to bathe and prepare to sleep. She was really tired; but felt safe and secure in her new home. She could hardly wait for tomorrow to write to her parents.

After breakfast and assisting with dishes, she hurried to her desk in her room and began to write.

"Dear Mom and Dad,
Thank you for your support. The train ride was great. I enjoyed seeing the countryside on the way to Fargo.
Mrs. Morgan, who is a lovely lady, met me at the station and brought me to the Crittenton Home. You would not believe what a huge clean place it is.
My roommate is Wanda. She is expecting her baby in July. Oh, is she large! I wonder if I will become that big.
I want to let you know that I am not afraid of the future.
Thanks, again, for loving me regardless of what has happened.
Your daughter, Harriet"

The social workers assisted Harriet in working with the Red Cross to locate Dave. They checked a number of places as his unit was on the move. At last, they found him on the front line near Germany. The Red Cross gave him the message about Harriet's new address because she was pregnant with his child.

About a month later, the Red Cross delivered a letter from Dave.

"Dear Harriet,
When your message arrived, I was shocked! I could not believe that you are pregnant. I am so sorry that you have to go through this alone.
I love you so much, Harriet. When I can get a furlough we shall get married. I want so much to have you as my wife. I am sorry we could not have married while I was at home, but then you would not have been able to finish high school. You know they do not want married girls in school.
The place you are living sounds wonderful. I am so glad you can go to a hospital for the birth of our baby. Just think, neither of our mothers had that opportunity. Good old Doc Thompson came to our homes to help with the births.
If our child is a boy, could you name him, 'James David;' if a girl, 'Elizabeth Harriet.' Thank you.
Remember, I will think about you each day. Take good care of yourself and our child.
Your sweetheart,
Dave"

The Home We Shared

The summer went quickly. She helped Wanda with preparations to go to the hospital. They talked often of their futures. Wanda's boyfriend was not interested in what had happened to her; thus, she had decided to give her child for adoption.

While Mrs. Morgan explained the procedure to Wanda, Harriet was encouraged to listen. "Three days after the birth of your child, Wanda, your baby will go to the North Dakota Children's Home. There the nurses will take very good care of your baby until the social workers have found the right parents for your baby." She continued, "Your child's background and appearance will be considered. They like to match the coloring of eyes, hair and complexion; but more than that, they want to match religious background and nationality."

Harriet was so glad she would not have to consider the possibility of adoption, as she and Dave would be married soon. She continued with the tasks assigned to her by the staff. She especially enjoyed cleaning the halls and stairs in the facility.

Wanda left for the hospital and the word was that she had a handsome boy. Mrs. Morgan said, "Wanda elected to not see or hold her child. She had family who took her back home from the hospital." Harriet prepared the bedroom for a new roommate.

A Red Cross Worker came to the front door and rang the doorbell. Harriet just happened to be cleaning the large entrance area so she answered the door. The person said, "I have a message for a 'Harriet....'"

Before she could complete her sentence, Harriet said, "I'm the only Harriet here. What is the message?"

The person handed her the telegram, and Harriet learned that Dave had been killed in action.

"Oh, no, no, no!" she screamed.

Mattie Morgan hurried out of her office and took the girl into her arms. "What is it, Harriet?"

"Dave has been killed," she sobbed, "We cannot get married, I will not have a husband, my child will not have a father! Oh, how awful!"

A few days later, a letter arrived from her mother.

"Dear Harriet,

I have very bad news for you. Dave's parents have just learned that he died in battle in France. They called to ask me to contact you. They will not have a funeral for him until the body can be brought back to Edgeley.

I did not tell them about his child. Everyone here thinks you went away to get a job. I am so sorry that your plans did not work out. Please think all of this through and let us know what you are going to do.

We love you so much,
  Mom and Dad"

The Home We Shared

St. John's Hospital.

Harriet's social worker spent many hours with her to assist her through these changes in her life. The news of Dave's death had destroyed her dream of raising the child in its own beautiful family!

After thinking it over for many weeks, Harriet made the difficult decision to place her child in an adoptive home. She signed papers stating that her baby would be taken to the North Dakota Children's Home. She knew that within two months after arriving there, the child would be adopted. As she wrote out the family history, she was very careful to get everything right — the nationalities, the religion, the health history, and educational background for two generations. Then, she did the same for Dave's side of the family.

In late November, Harriet gave birth to a beautiful little girl. It was so comforting to know she had the delivery staff at St. John's Hospital all working with her through the birth.

After she settled into her room, she asked the nurse, "May I hold my daughter for awhile?"

"Of course, you can. I'll go get her."

The nurse returned in a few minutes with the baby bundled in a pink blanket. On the child's wrist a bracelet of beads spelled out — "Baby Elizabeth."

"Dear child, I have to give you up. I want you to have two parents; I can give you only one." She sang to the child and kissed her forehead, "I love you so much and will always think about you. Please grow up to be a very special person."

Harriet held her for an hour. Then, she summoned the nurse. "I want you to take her back to the nursery."

The Home We Shared

Toddler Nursery at Children's Home, 1940.

To her baby she whispered, "Goodbye, my dear, Elizabeth."

In a few days, Elizabeth was taken to the Children's Home, and Harriet returned to the Crittenton Home. Harriet stayed until she had her strength back.

One day, a phone call came from her parents. They informed her that Dave's body had arrived in Edgeley and that the funeral would take place in a week.

The staff assisted her with packing, took her to the depot, and bought her train ticket. Mrs. Morgan wished her well and gave her a final hug near the passenger car.

"Thank you, Mrs. Morgan, you have helped me so much."

Harriet boarded the train that took her on the journey back home.

The funeral was most solemn. It was a bleak winter day. Harriet depended on her parents to get her through the service.

Since it was almost Christmas, she stayed with her family in the familiar old frame house on Main Street. How good it was to be home with her parents, to be with the people she loved and who loved her.

Despite all the warmth around her, her heart ached as she grieved two special people who had left her — the dear little baby, Elizabeth; and the young man, Dave.

Some days the grief was overwhelming, especially because she could not speak openly about her baby. On those days, she would seek out her parents and try to explain how she felt. When she wanted to share her grief over Dave, she could talk with her friends, family, and David's parents. She knew she must start a new life at age eighteen.

The Home We Shared

Baby Elizabeth

Baby Elizabeth entered the Home. Nurses in the Newborn Nursery cared for her 24 hours a day. The social workers immediately began the process of finding the right home for her.

Within two months, she was adopted by a couple who would raise her as their own child. They named her Anna Marie.

Factual Comments:

Nurses at the Home cared for three to eight newborn infants around the clock in the special Newborn Nursery. The nursery was on the second floor at the southeast corner. It was a bright room lined with windows on two sides. The metal cribs were along those two walls. It was directly above the room I shared with my parents.

Babies arrived from St. John's Hospital when they were three days old. They still wore their beaded wristbands with their names on them. When placed in their white cribs, a nurse clipped an identification card onto their bed.

The crib had a good mattress covered by a flannel sheet, a square of rubber cloth (to prevent dampness into the mattress), another sheet, and a small square of a thicker consistency. This top square could be changed more frequently when damp and provided the laundry with a smaller item to wash.

Babies "sunning" at the Home, 1930.

The Home We Shared

Next to the nursery, stood a complete examining room. It looked much like a doctor's office of the 1930s. Each day, a doctor came to check the infants. The doctor made recommendations concerning each child's care and charted the information.

Also daily, nurses weighed and bathed the infants. They dressed each baby in clean, white, tri-fold undershirts that tied in the front. They used the rectangular cotton diapers and, after about a week, added rubber pants so the bedding didn't get wet.

As the babies grew older, they wore cute rompers and jackets. In the cooler weather, they wore pastel colored sweaters and leggings. Always, they were covered with bright, flannel baby blankets.

When it was time for their feeding, a nurse brought from the Nursery Kitchen a slightly warmed bottle of formula made as the doctor had ordered. A caretaker rocked and fed each infant. The staff hoped that all of the babies would not want to be fed at the same time, and tried to keep the children on feeding times at least a half-hour apart. But, of course, the infants did not realize this; usually when one cried, another would wake. Often, the nursery staff would have to summon another nurse, aide, or one of the teenage girls living at the Home. After each feeding, the nurse charted what time the baby was fed and how many ounces the child drank.

Three children in jumper chairs.

The Newborn Nursery was a quiet and pleasant place. As a teenager, I spent many hours rocking and feeding the infants. We were all encouraged to talk and hum to the children as we fed them. I also assisted with the endless task of folding the clean baby-clothes.

Most infants were adopted before they reached the age of two months. If not, they simply moved to the Toddler Nursery in the next room to join other two-month to two-year-old children.

The Toddler Nursery was about five times the size of the Newborn Nursery. It had the same type of cribs lined up along two walls and a row or two in the center area. A large open area allowed the children to roll on the floor; use their jumper chairs; strollers, and swings; or play with toys. Here they learned to crawl and take their first steps.

A portion of the room was walled off to form the Nursery Kitchen. It had a Dutch door on it, so the children could be kept out of the kitchen for safety; but the workers could see what was happening in the nursery.

A large dressing room with two small, elevated bathtubs for caretakers to stand beside and bathe each child was attached to the Toddler Nursery. Nearby, another small room had a five-hole bench with slid-in potties, so more than one child could be potty trained at a time. This was one of my father's creations.

Across from the bench were many shelves to hold the clothes, bed sheets, and diapers for the toddlers. The diapers were the square flannel ones, which were folded in an "airplane design" to allow for more padding where most needed. The folding of these diapers took hours and hours.

The toddlers ate in highchairs or at small tables with chairs lined up near the kitchen. The nurses prepared many types of cereal, vegetables, fruit, and meat for the children. When they could give up their bottles, they were encouraged to drink from cups.

All of the toddlers were stimulated through touch and sound. The workers talked to them, held them, rocked them, and played with them on the floor. Music often filled the room.

These nurseries would have passed any modern day health standards.

Meal time in the Toddler Nursery.

Toddlers using the five-hole "potty chair."

The Home We Shared

Neglect and Abuse

Donna awoke with an aching sensation inside her body, and black and blue marks on the outside. She looked at her face in the small hand-held mirror near her mattress, asking herself, "How can I face the children today?"

She moved slowly to the edge of the bed and quietly slipped out onto the floor. This was all done quickly, as to not awaken Jeff, her husband. He breathed heavily in a deep sleep on the other side of the bed. She dressed in silence.

It was Sunday morning. Because of these new bruises, she knew she could not attend Holy Faith Assembly, but she would send the children. She knew that Reverend Boysen might stop during the week to inquire why Jeff and she were not in attendance, but for now this was the best she could do. Surely, by midweek the bruises on her face would lighten, and if she applied enough makeup, the minister would not notice them.

In the common area, used as a kitchen and living room, the four children rested on lumpy mats. Paula, Norton, Stephen, and Kelly all lay awake, but knew they should not make noise until their parents came out of the only bedroom. The children's faces showed they were relieved to see only their mother emerge from the side room.

Donna put her index finger to her puckered lips to give the "sh" sign. The children knew this meant to be VERY quiet. Without making a sound, the children stood up and walked to their "closet" which was a wooden apple crate standing on end. The crates offered two shelves as well as the top area for clothes storage.

Donna had carried the crates, one at a time, from the grocery store. Then, she took time to sort the bundle of clothes carried from their last apartment, placing them in each crate for the children. She liked this apartment on the second floor over a print shop. Donna thought it looked much neater than their last place.

The children pulled their Sunday clothes from the lower shelves and dressed. Then, they moved down the back stairway to use the outhouse.

Donna smeared a thin layer of peanut butter on five slices of bread. She placed them on yesterday's newspaper that lay on the table. Jeff must have brought it from the bar last night. "It was the only good thing that came from the bar," she thought.

As the children returned from the outhouse, Donna encouraged them to wash at the sink and to stand beside the table. She whispered a brief prayer and they all began to eat their slices of bread.

Then, she softly began her morning instructions, "Go directly to church. After Sunday school go to the worship service and sit up front. But, be quiet. When it is time to sing the praises, sing well as you know the songs." She continued, "If Reverend Boysen asks where your parents are, tell him your dad is ill and I stayed home to take care of him."

Paula, the oldest, said, "Mom, we'll be very good. I'll watch over the rest. May we stay for the cookies and punch after church?"

"Yes, Paula, that would be a good idea, but come home as soon as you have finished."

The children used the front stairway to get out to the sidewalk and went on their way to the church.

A couple hours later, the children returned. They were met at the bottom of the stairway by their mother, again, giving the "sh" sign. All day, whispers continued on the front stairway as Norton and Stephen played with a car, Kelly cuddled her doll and Paula read a book. They did not want to disturb their father.

About 3:00 P.M., they heard growling sounds from the bedroom. All froze in place, as they anticipated the appearance of " the man of the house."

"What's for supper?" he shouted as he slunk through the bedroom doorframe. "Hey, woman, get something on the table!"

Jeff walked to one of the two chairs at the table, sat down, and began to look at the newspaper. Without a word, Donna worked quickly at the stove as she prepared macaroni and cheese. She toasted the remaining slices of bread and applied peanut butter, again.

When all was readied, she asked the children to come stand at the table, each one in front of a dish of food. She sat on the remaining chair.

Jeff sat slumped forward in his chair and shoved the food into his mouth. At times, he would wipe his mouth with the back of his hand. "Where is the drink?" he grumbled.

"There isn't anything but water," replied Donna as she went to the faucet and filled a glass for him. She put a few more glasses on the table for the children and herself.

Everyone ate in silence.

Midweek, while the children were in school, the landlord arrived knocking soundly on the door of the apartment. "Mrs. Wilson, you owe two months of rent and now this month's rent is due. I cannot wait any longer. You'll have to pay immediately or get out!"

Donna was shocked. She had assumed Jeff had paid the rent on his paydays from working at the Cando Creamery. "I'll talk to my husband tonight. He must have forgotten to stop and pay you."

The landlord left in a huff slamming the door.

It was after 10:00 P.M., when Jeff stumbled up the stairs and into the apartment. Donna had already gone to bed and pretended to be asleep. She knew if she brought up the subject of the rent, there would be an argument and physical fight. Thus, she remained motionless and silent.

The next day after the children were at school, Jeff arose late. Donna said to him, "The landlord came yesterday. He says we owe three months of rent. Is that true?"

"Well, I forgot to pay it and I don't have the money now!"

"Best you look for a different place we can afford, as we'll have to move out right away," Donna said sullenly.

At 2 P.M., Jeff returned, "I've found a place for us! It is FREE! We will have to walk a mile out of town to reach it, but at least we will have a roof over our heads. Start packing!"

Donna stuffed their clothes into four gunnysacks she had carried potatoes in from the Corner Store. She placed food items and their few dishes into the sacks beside the clothes so they wouldn't break.

When the children came from school, she simply said, "Pick up your crates and come with us. We are moving."

The children saw that their belongings were gone, and lifted the crates up finding various ways to carry them. They started down the stairs following their dad and mom. Each of the parents carried two sacks. The children wondered where their next home would be.

The mile walk seemed more like ten to Donna and the children. Donna wondered what the "new place" would be like. As they rounded a curve in the road, straight-ahead was a dilapidated house. "Well, that can't be the place," she thought. "There is a big hole in the roof."

When he reached the house, Jeff turned into the yard. He continued walking around the house and towards a chicken coop. He pushed open the door and bent down to enter the coop. "Here we are," he said with authority. "I found this place this morning. No one will charge us to live here!"

Donna felt like running, but where would she go. "I think I will die," she thought. "The poor children will have to live in this dirt. How can I fix food?"

Without expressing any of her feelings to either Jeff or the children, she looked over the room and started preparing their home.

"Please leave everything outside, until I can sweep the floor."

"Fix it up," Jeff demanded, "and I'll see you later." He walked down the road towards the town. "I'll get Johnny to bring the mats, table, chairs, and our bed on his truck," he called back to the group.

Before long, Donna outlined in her mind where everything would go. The children would share the end of the coop by the door, so they could slip out to school or church without waking their father. Donna and Jeff's bed would be at the opposite end. The crates and clothes would be on the back wall so as not to shut off any of the light from the front windows.

"I still am not sure how to prepare the food," she thought. Then, she went outside to look around the yard. She found the screened-in back porch of the house in fair condition. Only a few holes in the screens and plenty of flies, but the roof seemed sturdy.

"Paula, please help me put the food and dishes in this area. When the table and chairs arrive, they will go here, too."

The two of them worked quickly, placing the items along the ledge where the screens met the wood frame.

"Come children; let's find some large stones or bricks to make a fire ring. Then, we will need to gather wood, so we can cook our meals outdoors."

Norton and Stephen ran to the field nearby and found some large rocks and carried them back to the yard. The fire ring was laid out about half way between the back of the old house and the chicken coop. Donna thought that would be the safest place for it.

Paula, Kelly and their mom brought sticks and branches to the area. As the children and she worked, Donna found an old pump over a cistern. "If I can prime it, we will at least have water for washing our clothes, dishes, and ourselves," she mused. "I must remember to have Jeff bring some water from town for us to drink and to prime the pump."

Late afternoon, a truck drove into the yard and Johnny and Jeff began to unload its contents. Donna directed them to place the table and chairs on the back porch. Then, she pointed out where the bed and mats should be placed.

"Please get a milk can of drinking water for us. I'll use a little to prime the pump, so we can wash in the cistern water," she directed the men. "I'll get the kids ready for bed. See you later."

She was relieved that she could prepare some food for their evening meal at the table. She realized they must be very hungry, but they never complained.

"Let's eat before it gets any darker. We only have one flashlight, so you must try to get to bed soon. I have your mats ready just inside the door. By morning sunlight, you should be able to dress."

Only a bit of moonlight assisted Jeff in finding his house. He stumbled across the room and fell onto the mattress. Again, Donna pretended to be asleep to avoid any confrontation.

"What will we do when it gets colder? How can we survive this move? Where will we get enough food?" All these questions rolled around in her head. Sleep came only in spurts.

A few days later, she had just sent the children on their walk to school. She was upset, as Jeff hadn't returned during the night.

She looked out the coop windows and saw a car moving along the road slowly. It passed by, but then slowly backed up, and turned into the driveway.

Donna did not move, "Maybe the person will leave. Surely, they would not believe that people are in this coop."

When the car door opened, Reverend Boysen stepped out. Without hesitation, he moved directly towards the coop. "He must know that we are living here," she thought. "Now, what do I do?"

The man knocked on the half-opened door and Donna went to meet him. She stepped outside, as there was no place inside to sit except on the mats.

"What are you doing here?" he asked in a soft voice. "I just now learned that Jeff had moved you to this coop."

"Yes, he did not pay the rent for three months, so we were kicked out of the other place."

"I came to tell you that Jeff was arrested this morning about 2:00 A.M. Some of the guys had been drinking and got into a big fight and broke store windows. Thus, the Towner County Sheriff has placed them in the jail."

"I wondered why he didn't come home last night," Donna said.

"Well, I was called in to talk with the fellows this morning. When I got to Jeff, I asked him where the family was. You see, last week, I had tried to visit you at your apartment and you were not there." Reverend Boysen continued, "I tried to find your family, but no one knew where you were living."

"This was all that Jeff could find. There isn't any money for rent. He spends it all on booze."

"Donna, I have to tell the county authorities what has happened to you and your children, as this is no way to raise children; nor is it a way for a woman to live. Donna, there are laws to protect your children. You will have to listen to the county people and abide by their suggestions."

Within a few hours, Donna was separated from her children as the sheriff took them to Fargo to the North Dakota Children's Home. She was encouraged to return to her parent's home in Bismarck.

Jeff would be spending some time in jail due to the destruction in town and for what he had done to his wife and children.

Factual Comments:

Abuse and neglect of family members has been happening for centuries. It was during the late 1800s that laws for the protection of children were written. More recently, laws to assist women (and men) in domestic violence situations have been developed.

While searching the history records of the Home, I came across numerous stories of abuse and neglect. In fact, one of the early stories tells of an unwed mother being pushed out of her parent's home and walking for miles in a snowstorm. Neither she nor her baby wore much clothing. She was assisted to the Home.

Also, there are many stories about women having to be placed in the Grafton Institution, a mental hospital. I wonder if it was due to postpartem blues, mental abuse by the spouse, or overwhelming circumstances that caused these women to have "mental problems." I can't imagine the extreme grief of having your children taken away — could this have made some "crazy?"

The fictitious story I created was based on one incident at the Home. I remember assisting my mom with cleaning up a family that had been brought in because they were found living in a chicken coop. I was so amazed, because regardless of how they lived, they wanted to be with their parents. That bond never seems to leave the children.

CRIPPLED CHILDREN'S PROGRAM AND SUMMER PROGRAM FOR THE CHILDREN'S HOME RESIDENT CHILDREN

...In a cabin out on the North Dakota Badlands, a child with a deformity is born. The midwife and the parents feel that the child will have to live the best he can with the physical disorder. Many walk for years with an awkward gait due to congenital hip conditions and clubbed feet.

...While assisting with planting and harvesting on the prairie fields, a child loses an arm or foot as he becomes entangled in the farm equipment. Either a doctor is summoned from a distance or the child is rushed by buggy or farm truck to the nearest medical person. Little can be done and the child must live with the handicap.

... A child is severely burned when playing with matches. Her burns are taken care of with butter or an ointment. They never heal properly and the child is scarred for the rest of her life.

... A crippling disease, such as polio, causes physical changes in a child's body. The family assists the child to live with the handicap.

... Other children have poor eyesight, clef pallets, harelips, speech impediments such as stuttering, or hearing problems. These children try to fit into their communities and schools, but find rejection.

The Crippled Children's Program was developed in 1921 to assist these special North Dakota children. This program would also involve the staff and children of the North Dakota Children's Home.

Two summer residents at the Home, 1930.

The Home We Shared

Factual Comments:

In 1936, the Social Security Act created a fund for the "Crippled Children." The State-Federal Child Welfare Services Program set aside a greater amount of money to be used for the special children.

In 1937, the Federal Social Security Act gave a sum of $29,000 and the State of North Dakota contributed $22,000 towards the treatment of crippled children. The Elk's Club organization traveled the state to find the children who were handicapped. Their survey revealed 1,500 North Dakota children needed medical treatment and/or some type of surgery.

During the summer months, the Elks Club gave individualized care to these special children through the "Crippled Children's Summer Program." The medical communities of Fargo, North Dakota, Minneapolis, Minnesota, and Rochester, Minnesota, joined the Elks by donating diagnostic and surgical services. The children were housed in the North Dakota Children's Home for both pre- and post-surgery treatments.

Crippled Boy, 15, Sees First Movie in Fargo

Engelbert Volk will return to St. Luke's hospital in a day or two for another operation and a dreary period of convalescence flat on his back, but at the end of that time the hopes to be able to walk on his two feet a well as any other 15-year-old boy; and meanwhile he has the memory of the most glamorous evening he's ever know to carry him through.

Friday night Engelbert saw his first motion picture, attending, "Footlight Parade" in the Fargo theater as the guest of Manager Ed Kraus.

Engelbert is the son of Mr. and Mrs. George Volk, farmers near Selfridge. He was born with one leg not quite as it should be, and for a good many years there haven't been many pleasures open to him, what with the difficulty of getting around on two crutches. He's already spent several weeks in St. Luke's hospital, and he faces his return there with fortitude, confident this operation "won't go so bad." His trip to Fargo from Selfridge was the first time he had been on a train.

About the movie, it is Engelbert's private opinion James Cagney was the whole show. The music left Engelbert a bit cold, but he admitted he had no ear for music.

Engelbert, fourth youngest in a family of 11 children, would just as soon as not make Fargo his permanent home after seeing "Footlight Parade," streetcars and the glittering red and blue lights of Broadway shops, he's not a bit discontented on the farm, because, he says, he's gone into business for himself and is the personal caretaker of 23 head of sheep and 9 cattle.

Engelbert acquired a good share of his stock by acting as a volunteer nursemaid and amateur veterinarian for sick and wounded young pigs, sheep or calves.

"Neighbors would give me a sick pig," he said, "And I'd take care of it. Or they'd give me a sick calf. Some of them died, but the ones that lived were mine.'

He sold some of his stock, and with the proceeds bought more. One piglet he raised to maturity from a bad beginning curried out a capable mother and presented him with a large litter.

In order to accommodate these special children, about 25 to 30 "resident children" were moved from the Fargo facility to lake cottages near Detroit Lakes, Minnesota

The first summer, 200 patients were accepted to the Crippled Children's Program and 104 of these children lived at the North Dakota Children's Home Society.

The Home We Shared

Mr. Bond states in the 1938 Annual Report, "This means hundreds of trips to hospitals, clinics, stores, and to and from trains. From 5 o'clock in the morning until 11:30 at night the house staff was busy. They deserve honorable mention for this willing service."

The Knight's Summer Home

Orphans Had the "Grandest Time" As Guests of Knights

Wesley Grins From Ear-To-Ear In Memory of Gala Vacation At West Cormorant Summer Home

By ALMA RIGGLE

"We have been to the lakes-it was swell-for three days, too-we had fireworks and cherries-and apples and ice cream"

Wesley, 7, began talking before he climbed into his chair for an interview and you really ought to hear him tell it. We can't do his enthusiasm justice and the great big grin that showed his half-grown new incisors and the way he hugged himself in pure delight at the memory of the best time in his young life can't be described.

Nina, 13, echoed Wesley's enthusiasm when they came to The Fargo Forum office to tell about the annual outing of the North Dakota Children's home society at the summer home of Mr. and Mrs. Fred Knight on West Cormorant. Mr. and Mrs. Knight yearly are hosts to all of the children from the society who can go at the time. They keep them at the lake for three days and make the occasion more than even the fondest dreams of childhood.

"We didn't have to ask for anything. Mr. Knight said we didn't," Wesley said and then painted an alluring picture of the goodies that you just helped yourself to whenever you felt like it.

"'Course, Robert's stomach ached," he admitted. "Too much candy — I like the cherries best. We all got presents. I got a bow and arrow and a top. Atis got a parasol. She (Nina) got a bracelet and ear rings: Mary's ring has her initials on it. Gladys had to stay home, 'cause she had chicken pox, but Miss Bond brought her a doll and a parasol."

'My They're Good'

"My but Mr. Knight is a good man," Nina paid tribute to her benefactor from the wisdom of her 13 years. "And Mrs. Knight is a good woman," she added hastily.

"There ain't nobody else like them," Wesley interposed, He doesn't always say "ain't" but you know how it is.

From the youngsters' stories of the outing, it was an occasion surpassing even those the Knights have given in previous years. They were without restriction, played on grassy lawns, rolled down embankments, went swimming in the cool lake waters, boat rides any time they cared to (one boat leaked and it was an important moment when the young passengers helped the man in charge row to shore), ate to their heart's content and their tummies in distress, went to bed as tired as tired could be, rolled out in the morning all agog. They saw a two-hour program of fireworks Thursday night, went fishing for real fish a time or two in a synthetic fish pond that yielded each one or more gifts during the last day of their stay and came home just about the happiest children you ever saw.

To provide room for this service, the resident children and staff traveled to the lake for the summer. From 1930-1938, they were housed at the "Holiday House Episcopal Church Camp" on Pelican Lake for two weeks. This was due to the kindness of the Episcopal Church Group, Bishop J. Pointz Tyler, and Bishop Bartlett. Later, they stayed at Camp Watson on Pelican Lake, making room for many more "crippled children" to stay on at the Home.

Now that there was space at the Home in Fargo, children from all parts of North Dakota spent the summer at the Children's Home. The Fargo doctors and specialists determined the needs of each child with the hope of completing the treatments by the end of the summer. When these children returned to their hometowns, their local doctors

Holiday House Episcopal Church Camp, 1933.

Children at the Fred Knight Cottage, West Cormorant, 1920s.

Party at the Knight's Cottage, 1920s.

cared for them. Many of these children made the trip to Fargo numerous summers.

The Home staff became the "summer parents" to these children, encouraging and supporting them through the pain and fear of their surgery. Often, the two men on staff carried the patients up the steep stairs to their beds for the night, and down the stairs in the morning.

All other workers became post surgery nurses. They took care of dressings and treatments between the doctors' visits. This was at a time when the only handicap devices available were wheelchairs and crutches. No walkers, high toilet seats, lift bars on walls, or electric positioning beds were available to assist with their care.

The Elks gave time and added funds to the Social Security money to continue the Crippled Children's Program. Counties assisted with board and room at the North Dakota Children's Home, as these were expenses that, often, their families could not afford.

This was a wonderful program for the children of the rural parts of North Dakota. How proud the staff of the Home was to be a part of this summer health program. Through the years, they observed the children developing into healthy young men and women. Elk Club Members, the medical personnel, and the Home staff did a great medical service during those years.

The Crippled Children's Summer Program assisted thousands of children with their ailments, and at the same time, gave the resident children from the Home great opportunities to enjoy Camp Watson. There they played in the sun and experienced the great outdoors for three months.

As we came into the 1970s, early detection, modern medical knowledge, and early surgery, eliminated many physical handicaps, so the Crippled Children's Program was no longer necessary. It was a great program in its time and the Home staff participated with all their energy and concern.

Camp Watson

Mr. Harold H. Bond writes in his Annual Report to North Dakota Children's Home Society on December 31, 1938.

"A real need of your Society had been a better summer plan for the children. With a large number of crippled children to be cared for during June, July, and August, we have had to make other plans for about 25 of the older boys and girls. The past two years we rented cottages at a lake in Minnesota. This worked rather well as shown by the increased good health of the children when they returned in the fall. The renting plan, however, is not so satisfactory as we have needed a place of our own where improvements made would be lasting and be credited to the Society. We are happy to report that this need is about to be realized."

The Home We Shared

In 1938, Mrs. J. S. Watson purchased a large cottage on Pelican Lake with five lots on Midland Beach from two Canadians. She, in turn, gave it to the Children's Home in the name of her late husband, Mr. Watson, a former Jamestown lawyer. Thus, "Camp Watson" was established on Pelican Lake and used by the Children's Home from 1939-1960. Mr. Bond reported, *"Last year (1939), 40 children spent several weeks at the lake, 20 of these for the full three months."*

Mrs. Watson's daughter, Mrs. James W. Pollock, provided a gift of $300.00 per year for 20 years to maintain the cottage and grounds. When the 20 years came to an end in 1959, Camp Watson was a well-kept modern and beautiful facility, and was licensed by the Minnesota Department of Health and Sanitation.

Harold H. Bond dedicated his Annual Report to the Society on December 31, 1946 to Mrs. J. S. Watson, who died March 7, 1946.

"Mrs. Watson became a member of the Board of Directors of this Society in 1917 and served faithfully since that time (total of 29 years). She loved children and gave generously to meet the needs of the Society. She purchased and equipped Camp Watson on Pelican Lake, Minnesota, and provided for its future upkeep. She remembered the Society in her many bequests to charitable, educational and religious institutions. The staff and children of the North Dakota Children's Home Society have lost a good friend.

"All the older boys and girls spent $2^1/_2$ months at our fine cottage at Pelican Lake in the summer. This was a wonderful opportunity to have them outdoors most of the time and in the water several times every day.

"Thinking of the splendid use to which Camp Watson has been put, we cannot help but think of the woman who made that all possible, Mrs. J. S. Watson, to whom this report is dedicated. She loved children, wanted to do something for those unfortunate ones that would build them up in

Cottage at Camp Watson, east side — back door.

body and mind and so we have one of the best small camps to be found. Here every year the children of the Society spend weeks and months in outdoor life and come back ready for school and ready for whatever may come their way."

Cottage at Camp Watson, west side — front door, 1950.

Cottage at Camp Watson, south side — Pelican Lake.

The Home We Shared

The Home We Shared

History of the Home
Told through the stories of the people intimately involved

Andrew Horace Burke
Reverend E.P. Savage
Reverend C.J. McConnehey
Reverend B.H. Brasted

Reverend Frank "Daddy" Hall
Laura Rundle
Dr. C.J. Dillon
Lucy J. Babcock Hall
Harold H. Bond
Robert C. Olslund
Mabel Miller
Miss Jean Love
Miss Elizabeth Wells
Remembering Some of the Other Workers
Esther Hartvickson
Mrs. Laybourne
Mrs. Raines
"Hansie" the Cook
Miss Graffee
Miss Gray
Mr. & Mrs. Peter Waldera

The Home We Shared

Andrew Horace Burke

As the governor of North Dakota in the late 1800s, Andrew Burke played a significant role in starting the North Dakota Children's Home Society. His background (excerpted here from "Burke's Journey's" by Dorothy Lund Nelson; Illustrations by Howard Ralston, formerly of Petersburg, ND) explains his passion for children arriving in North Dakota on the orphan trains.

During the year of 1850, Mr. and Mrs. Burke, a young couple from Ireland, were excited to learn they were expecting their first child. Mrs. Burke was in poor health during her pregnancy and as the days neared for her child to be born, she became extremely ill. She died as she gave birth to a lanky, red-haired boy on May 15.

Mr. Burke experienced many emotions while preparing for his wife's burial. Joy and pleasure engulfed him because of his baby son, who he proudly named, "Andrew Horace Burke." Tears filled his eyes due to his overwhelming sadness over the loss of his loving wife.

The first years for "Andy" were difficult. While his papa worked in the factory, various people in the apartment took turns caring for him. Mr. Burke worked many long days; but, when he returned home, he always took time for his child. In 1854, when Andrew was only four years old, his papa died very unexpectedly.

On Andy's fifth birthday, his caretakers stated, "You must go to work to earn your board and keep. Go out tomorrow and find a job."

Andy knew that he must look for work and then pay to live in their home. It didn't take long for Andy to find a job: it was as a paperboy. From an assigned corner in the huge city, he sold THE TRIBUNE newspaper published by Horace Greeley.

The Home We Shared

A few years later, Andrew was placed in the Randall Island Orphanage. From there, in 1858, Charles Loring Brace encouraged him and other boys to ride one of the "Orphan Trains" to the West with Mr. Macy. Andrew's train went to Noblesville, Indiana.

As Mr. Macy led them on a short walk to the Christian Church, Andy noticed that it was a bright and sunny day. Entering the church, the boys found a large congregation gathered to look them over. Before long, many of the boys were shaking hands with sets of parents.

Andrew and John were standing there alone! Andy thought, "Will John and I be the "leftovers?" Andrew tried to look even more pleasant by putting on a big smile.

Moving towards Andy was a man who reached out his large hand to him. Andrew thought, "He looks like the richest man I have ever seen."

Soon, the man was talking to him, "Hello, young man, I am Mr. D. W. Butler. My wife and I live on a farm in the country." Andy listened carefully as Mr. Butler went on to say, "We would like very much to have you join our family."

Andrew beamed. "Mr. Butler, I would like to be part of your family," he said with a nervous giggle in his voice. Mr. Butler shook Andrew's hand. Then, the boy took off his hat and gave a little bow to the gentleman.

THE HOME WE SHARED

Suddenly, Andy thought about John Brady. Out of the corner of his eye, he saw that John was walking across the platform with an elegant gentleman.

Andrew learned later, when they attended school together, that John's newfound father was a lawyer named Mr. John Green. John told Andy that his father decided to give the boy part of his name, so now his name was, "John Green Brady."

Andy, now an eight-year-old boy, held tightly to the hand of his new father. He skipped fast beside Mr. Butler to keep up with his long strides. They hurried along the dirt road to the hitching post where the horse and wagon waited for them.

Many things happened in the following years. Andy was in the Civil War; later, he received a good education, and moved farther West to work in Minneapolis and New York Mills, Minnesota He eventually settled in Casselton, North Dakota.

In November 1890 the people of North Dakota went to the polls with a choice between three candidates for governor. When the ballots were counted, Andrew H. Burke had overwhelmingly won the election. He became the second Governor of North Dakota; John Miller, the "Territorial Governor," was the first governor.

On the blustery, winter day of January 7, 1891, Andrew walked onto a stage wrapped in red, white, and blue bunting. There, he placed his left hand on the Bible, raised his right hand, and repeated an oath. Thus, he was sworn in as Governor of North Dakota.

The Home We Shared

Once he became governor, it didn't take long for Burke to lobby for the welfare of children. He convinced the legislators to write and pass laws for the welfare and adoption of children in North Dakota. In 1891, with the guidance of Reverend Savage of the Minnesota Children's Home Society, Burke established an auxiliary to take care of the neglected and destitute children living within the state and the many "leftovers" from the Orphan Trains arriving frequently in the state. Years later, records show that 975 Orphan Train Riders were "placed out" in North Dakota by the New York Children's Aid Society. Also, the New York Foundling Hospital sent many children to Catholic families.

The auxiliary started collecting money for the home and Reverend C.J. McConnehey became the first Superintendent. Until the Home was built in 1892, McConnehey often took the children to his own home to live until they could be placed into a new home. The Home burned to the ground in the city's great fire of 1893. For a few years the Home was relocated in Grand Forks. One hundred and fifty-seven children were cared for under Reverend McConnehey's leadership.

In 1995, Reverend McConnehey left North Dakota and Reverend Brasted became the second Superintendent. With his leadership a new Children's Home was built at 804 10th Street South in Fargo and opened in 1900. It would be the Home for over 9,000 children until 1957. Reverend Brasted assisted two hundred and forty-two children in seven years.

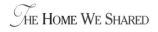
The Home We Shared

From "Fargo Argus" — June 7, 1894

"A Worthy Charity"
The North Dakota Children's Home Society.

"Help a child to find a home."

Among Fargo's many eleemonsynary institutions none are more worthy than the children's home. Supt. McConehey writes thus of the home:

"The mission of the home is to seek homeless, neglected, and destitute children and become their friend and protector: to place them, with the least possible delay, in approved families; to protect society, by guaranteeing proper home training and education to the unfortunate little ones — against its greatest enemies, Ignorance and Vice and thus improve American citizenship.

By the employment of active agents, local advisory boards, district and state superintendents, and a general superintendent, a thorough supervision is kept over all our children. Continued abuse or neglect of a child under this system is impossible.

'Help a child find a home.'"

THE HOME WE SHARED

FRANK DREW HALL
Better known as "Daddy Hall"

In 1902, Frank "Daddy" Hall became the Superintendent of the Children's Home, initiating a period of great energy, growth, and change. As superintendent, he participated in the first White House Conference for Dependent Children in 1909; fought vigorously for the Mother's Pension Law (precursor to Aid for Dependent Children) in 1915; and in 1923 was a member of North Dakota's Children's Code Commission. Through these events and other activities, he influenced significant legislation for the protection of children.

In the final year of the 24 years of Hall's leadership, North Dakota Children's Home records indicated a responsibility for 250 children in the orphanage and in boarding and foster care.

In the following excerpts from his autobiography, Hall tells of his days at the North Dakota Children's Home Society.

Off to Dakota for Good

Many years ago, Horace Greeley advised young men to go west and grow up with the country. It has been fortunate for me that my "best girl" went west, for she certainly was the magnet that pulled me away from low-paid labor in the east (Ohio) and introduced me to a new career in North Dakota, which had just become a state.

We (Nellie Maud Hart and Frank Drew Hall) were married in the parlor of Will and Stella (Nellie's sister) McKinstry's home at four o'clock in the afternoon of Nell's 22nd birthday, June 14, 1890. Reverend J.M. Davis, pastor of the First Baptist Church, tied the knot and Reverend McKnight, pastor of First Methodist Church assisted.

Opening of the home, 1900.

The Home We Shared

Our first son, Jeremiah Lawrence, was born April 25, 1891, about five minutes before midnight. He was named for his great-grandfather, Dr. Jeremiah Hall, and for his maternal grandfather, Daniel Lawrence Hart.

Our second son, Donald Fletcher Hall was born in 1896.

The Work for Homeless Children

After almost 10 year's service as Sunday school missionary in Dakota, I began to feel that it was unfair to my wife to put upon her all the responsibility of training our children to useful manhood. I was away from home a large part of the time. When in the Black Hills, more than a thousand miles away, my heart was hungry for home life and Nell longed to have me with the family, although she never interposed any objection to my absence while in Sunday school work. My two boys were at an age when they needed a father as well as a mother.

In the spring of 1902, it seemed as if Providence was opening the way to a realization of our dreams. For some time past, the Ladies' Auxiliary of the North Dakota Children's Home Society, at Fargo, had been dissatisfied with some of the features of the work as carried on by Superintendent B.H. Brasted. My relations with him had always been pleasant, so far as we came in contact. As the Ladies had solicited all the funds with which the Receiving Home was built and were doing much to maintain the home, they finally asked Mr. Brasted to resign as Superintendent. This seemed to sour him, and he felt very bitter at the treatment accorded him. He had been Superintendent for seven years, succeeding Reverend McConnehey, who filled the office for a year and a half.

One day in the early spring, Mrs. Tom L Sloane, one of the most active of the ladies, approached me, told me they expected to make a change of superintendent, and asked me if I would consider taking it over. I told her I would do nothing that could be interpreted as opposing Mr.

Mrs. Thomas F. Sloan, one of our most active workers for the home. "The Home finder" will be distributed at the (state) fair (in Mandan) by Mrs. Sloan, who is a veritable "home finder" herself.

The Home We Shared

Brasted, but that if he gave up the work I might then consider it. A few days later she informed me that he had resigned, and would leave about May 20 for California. On behalf of the Society she again urged me to accept the position now vacant. I told her I was bound to the work of the American Baptist Publication Society, but if they would release me I would accept the position on a basis of $1,200 a year salary, and out of it would meet my own traveling expenses. The Publication Society accepted my resignation, but requested me to attend to the field correspondence until a successor could be found. I became superintendent of the Home Society on May 20, 1902, my 38th birthday.

On my return to Fargo, I found the Ladies' Auxiliary in full force at the Home. In my absence they had raised and installed four hundred dollars' worth of furniture, rugs, dishes, curtains, and other furnishings, and the Home began to look more cheerful. They had done this as a housewarming for us, and it certainly helped the situation.

As we had no intention of giving up our own home, I engaged Mrs. Jennie A. Benedict, widow of a former Northern Pacific engineer, as matron of the Home. Mrs. Benedict had been Matron in the Michigan State Home at Coldwater. She was taken very ill after she had served [at the North Dakota Children's Home] for six months, and resigned her work. My good wife then assumed the matronship, and Mrs. Nellie Hyatt, of Pelican Rapids, Minnesota, became assistant matron. She had filled a similar position in a home in New Jersey. She was a trained nurse in army hospitals in England, obeyed instructions strictly, and was a valuable worker.

About this time an epidemic of dysentery struck our nursery, and before it could be checked, swept away fourteen babies. We shall never forget the trying experiences of those trying days. Nell never got over the shock of so many deaths, and to this day the wrinkles on her forehead tell the story of sleepless nights of anxious watching. Only when the nursery was emptied of its homeless charges did the epidemic cease, although many Fargo physicians did all they could to find the source of the trouble and kill the scourge.

(The Halls adopted their daughter, Clara, a one-year-old child, in 1902)

After six months as matron, Nellie turned over her work to Mrs. Hyatt, who retained it for four years (1906), when she married a well-to-do farmer named Rich, from Detroit (Lakes), Minnesota Their wedding took place in the parlor of the Home.

During the early part of our service with the Home, Mrs. W. H. Hunt and Mrs. Morton Page, of the Auxiliary, made a tour of the state soliciting funds for the installation of a hot-water heating plant for the Home. This was a great help to the work. A little later the same ladies persuaded Honorable R. M. Pollock, of Fargo, to prepare a bill for presentation to the Legislature, providing a biennial appropriation of $3,000.00 from the state treasury in support of the Home. The measure was not engineered by the Society, and the board of directors knew nothing of the ladies' intentions until the bill had been introduced. The women lobbied effectively, and the measure passed both houses with no opposition, but the Governor, Honorable Frank White, vetoed it on the ground that it was unconstitutional.

It was fortunate that he did so. It was entirely contrary to the practice of other state members of the National Children's Home Society, which had never solicited state aid, for fear it would throw the work into politics. Beside this feature, it would have killed charity from the general public. Had we received $3,000.00 every two years from the state treasury it would have gone but a small way toward the total amount needed, and the balance would still have to be raised by public charity.

Some of the board members felt otherwise, and the ladies who engineered the bill never since have assisted in raising funds. Mrs. Hunt, however, always remained interested in needy children, and on numerous occasions gave me valuable assistance.

Upon becoming superintendent I began the publication of a monthly paper called, "The Children's Home Finder." A year or so later it was changed to a 16- to 20-page bi-monthly magazine, and has ever since been the official organ of the Society. For a year or two I set the type myself and had it printed by Brown and Gage. After quitting this task under the pressure of more important work, the printing job was turned over to Walker Brothers and Hardy.

Mrs. Hyatt was succeeded in the Matron's position by a Mrs. Shaw, a very nice, motherly women — really too old for the work involved. She held on for a year or more and turned the place over to a Mrs. McLeod, wife of an insane Presbyterian missionary. It became necessary to fire her for unbecoming conduct and conspiracy. A trained nurse, Miss Pearl Carey, followed Mrs. McLeod. I had met Miss Carey in St. Paul when she was assistant matron of the Minnesota Children's Home Society. She served four years and then entered the Salvation Army.

The death of our son Lawrence, on April 2, 1909, was a tremendous blow to us and cast a shadow over our lives that has remained ever since. He had been

Frank "Daddy" Hall

married the previous fall to Miss Lucy Babcock, daughter of S.B. and "Mittie" Babcock — close Baptist friends of ours. Lawrence was working for the Scott Hall shoe store in Fargo when he contracted pneumonia, and slipped away in a coma five days later. His posthumous son was born a few weeks later in our home. He was named Lawrence Babcock Hall. Lucy, who never remarried in all these years, has done a wonderful work in raising this fine lad, who promises to become a fine, upstanding man.

Nell has continued much of the time as matron and for some years we made our home in the little cottage adjoining the receiving home. Donald graduated from high school in 1913 and the following fall entered Fargo College.

Many hundreds of homeless children have been cared for in the Home since we took over the work, and Nell has been the only mother many of them had known before coming here. Most of our wards were placed in Christian homes, to become useful members of their new families. This function — the placement of children with Christian families — has been the great work of my life.

A Piano for the Home

The date is not known, but I found the story amid newspaper articles clipped long ago and placed in a scrapbook. It was from these news stories that I learned about the piano that was located in the staff dining room. They stated that the Stone Music House of Fargo had decided to donate two pianos, a Victor and a Kimball, to a local organization. The owners created a contest in which people could vote on which was most deserving of the piano. During a period of time, persons marked their ballots and the numbers were tallied.

One Newspaper article reported:

"The friends of the Catholic Orphanage continue to make big gains in the Kimball piano voting contest and this week starts out a notch higher, having passed the Children's Home. The hook and ladder boys gained 99,000 votes, the Elks 101,000, The Children's Home 88,000."

Finally, the voting was closed on a Monday afternoon at 1:00 P.M. At that time the votes stood at, "Company B — 1,127,990; Catholic Orphanage — 25,374; Children's Home — 11,523; Minot High School — 12. It is needless to say that the members and officers of the successful company are feeling much gratified at the outcome of the contest and appreciate the efforts of their friends."

But, there must have been some disagreement between the Elks and the Rescue Company as to which group was the final winner. Thus, the newspaper printed this well-written letter from "A Lady." It was so well written that it did change the results of where the piano would be placed.

"Since the Elks and the Rescue Boys appear to have gotten into a controversy over the contest for the Kimball piano, why would it not be a noble and proper thing for them to give the piano to the Children's Home? This is the only organization that was a candidate for the piano, which really is in need of one, as I understand. The Yerxa's have a piano in their parlors and the members of the Rescues can enjoy its music. There is a piano in Elks hall, which the Elks can use.

A piano at the Children's Home would be such a pleasant thing for the little children, not that they should be allowed to play it or in fact touch it, but that they might enjoy the music. We often have lady visitors who would be glad to play a few selections for the entertainment of the children and rather than have any unpleasantness caused between the Elks and the Rescues, I think they should agree to allow the piano to be given to the Home. Ask the boys to think it over."

The next news article stated:
"Contest Settled"

"At a meeting last evening between representatives of the Elks and the Rescue Hook and Ladder Association, it was finally decided to settle the differences between the organizations in the matter of the recent Kimball piano voting contest, by both parties waiving claims to the piano and having it turned over to the Children's Home. This amicable way of settling the dispute will be noted with pleasure by all interest in the same, especially when the piano will go to so worthy a cause as that of the North Dakota Children's Home Association. All the organizations in the contest wish to thank George Wasem for his fairness in caring for the matters of the contest and for his just dealings with participants in the same."

"That Piano"

By Frank D. Hall: The Children's Home Society has not been officially notified by the Elks and Rescues that they desired to compromise matters by presenting the Kimball piano contested for by them to the Children's Home; but on behalf of the Society and the children at the Home I can assure these gentlemen that such a gift will scarcely be declined. In fact, we are very happy over the prospects of having this instrument for use at family worship and at other times in the Home.

The Home made a hard fight last winter to secure the piano that was finally won by the G.A.R., but were glad to see the old soldiers win — If we could not.

When the Victor and Kimball pianos were put up for contest, we publicly announced we would like to see the Co. B. boys get the Victor, as they had asked for it. We went into the contest for the Kimball because we needed the instrument and were unable to buy one, but got swamped in the effort to keep up with the Rescues and the "Best People On Earth." They had facilities for vote getting that we could not compete with, and

The Home We Shared

we early saw our undoing.

However, "the race is not always to the swift, nor the battle to the strong," and these strong organizations have done the graceful thing by compromising on the Home. Accepting the newspaper reports as correct, we can only extend to the Elks and Rescues our heartfelt thanks for this generous gift to the Home."

More Words from Frank D. Hall's Autobiography

Special Recognition

My recognition as an expert in this field was recognized in the first decade of my work. I was invited by President Theodore Roosevelt to come to the White House, where he had arranged a conference on the care of dependent children.

The invitation caused quite a commotion in Fargo. I was given wide publicity. I, of course, accepted and Nell and I made the trip to Washington. There, with other workers similarly qualified, we were received in a special meeting at the White House and cordially greeted by the President. Later, during the conference, we attended the big banquet at the Willard Hotel, at which the President was the principal speaker. It was a great adventure in our comparatively humble lives.

Bit of Philosophy

So, I near the end of my story, in the year 1916. I am only 52 years of age, so it seems probable that I will have a good many years yet to live. It seems highly probable that I will end my days in the type of work which has brought me the most satisfaction — the work for the homeless

Frank D. Hall and three young clients. From 1902 until 1927, Mr. Hall was a tireless spokesman for child welfare. These are "leftover children" from an orphan train that stopped in Fargo.

child. Since being made a Juvenile Court Commissioner, in addition to my regular work with the Home, my field of activity has expanded, but it all centers about the welfare of children.

Conclusion of Frank D. Hall's Autobiography
(Prepared by Donald F. Hall, son of Frank Hall)

The great humanitarian work of my father continued in the field of help to homeless children until 1926, when in the spring of the year he was stricken with apoplexy which completely paralyzed his side and made him an invalid for the remaining 11 years of his life.

While the work of the Children's Home continued satisfactorily, and Dad received several increases in salaries, as living costs became higher, the post-war period brought on new worries. The most pressing of these grew out of efforts by eastern politicians, to regulate and standardize the work of placement agencies throughout the country. The fiscal aspects of new regulatory provisions precipitated many a financial crisis in the work and involved tremendous problems that eventually brought on the stroke.

For a month or two the outcome of the attack was in doubt, but it soon became apparent that many years of complete helplessness lay ahead of the patient. It was finally decided that he and Mother (Nell) would go to California, where my sister, Clara, and her husband, Dr. John D. Keye, were about to set up a small hospital at Holtville, in the southern part of the state. Mother had been sufficiently experienced to be considered an excellent practical nurse, and the arrangement gave Dad

The receiving cottage was moved to back of the Home so the addition could be added on the right side, 1912–1914.

The Home We Shared

("Daddy Hall") the opportunity for hospitalization, with some income for Mother. The plan worked for some years, but the heat and a change of plans on the part of Clara and Doctor John resulted in Mother and Dad coming to our home in Kokomo, where we all lived together for a couple of years.

About 1935, Mother's Aunt Angeline Cole, in Geneva, Ohio, invited the folks to come and live with her. They took up residence in the old hometown where they had first met.

Dad's condition gradually weakened until June 24, 1937. I was at my desk at the Kokomo Tribune, (Indiana) when a telegram came stating that I would have to hurry if I wanted to see my father alive. Nina and I took off by car at once and in six hours drove up in front of the Geneva home. Mother came running to the door as I arrived, hurrying us into the house just in time to kneel by my father's bed as he died.

We laid Dad away in the little plot in the cemetery just a stone's throw from where he died. After his death my mother lived for some years with Aunt Angie in her Cleveland, Ohio, apartment, and took care of Aunt Angie's daughter, Ivy Cole Weld, prior to her death. Aunt Angie died a few years later, leaving Mother with an annuity that has met her financial needs ever since.

Mother continued to live in the house at 257 Walnut Street in Geneva, until September of 1955, when her extreme age and infirmity required much personal care. We brought her to our home here in Orlando, where she has nothing to do but bask in Florida's wonderful sunshine. She is nearing 89 years of age as I write.

It was in preparing for the sale of the Geneva house, which Nina and I bought in 1948, that Nina found the manuscripts of Dad's autobiography, from which I have typed this chronicle.

The End

Excerpts from "Autobiography of Frank Drew Hall, 1864-1937"
Edited from his hand-written manuscript by his son,
Donald Fletcher Hall — completed on March 16, 1957

Fundraisers

When the North Dakota Children's Home was incorporated, it was set up to be funded by individual donors rather than be supported by the North Dakota State treasury. Thus, many types of fundraisers were designed to tell the story to all individuals in the state.

North Dakota State Fair

The first public fundraising event for the North Dakota Children's Home was in 1902 at the State Fair located at Mandan. The booth had "Children's Home Finder" newsletters available and many photographs of the children. Mrs. Thomas F. Sloan, Associate President for the Ladies' Department of the fair, took the responsibility of distributing the newsletters and talking to people about the needs of children. She suggested that each person give financial gifts to the Home.

In 1912, at the State Fair in Fargo, the Home workers decorated a booth (9x24 feet) in the balcony of the Agricultural Building. Staff and three to ten children occupied the booth each day. The "Children's Home Finder" of August 15th, 1912 states:

"The Home booth was tastefully arranged as a nursery on a small scale, with cribs, children's chairs, toys and many pictures from the Home. This booth proved to be one of the greatest drawing cards of the fair during the hours when the children were there.

Each afternoon at 2 o'clock babies and nurses were brought in hacks and remained till 5 o'clock. The Home children looked neat and attractive. — Women would stand and watch the babies until tears filled their eyes, and more than one strong man wiped his eyes as he turned away to think of his own happy children, or of some baby plucked like a flower by the Grim Reaper in bygone days."

"Children's Home Day"
1904 until 1921 and possibly longer

Around 1904, Daddy Hall inaugurated a special "Day," which later became a week for raising funds and food through the North Dakota School systems. The Friday before Thanksgiving was designated as "Children's Home Day." Hall mailed large posters and other information to the schools. Children across the state brought their coins to school to help the children of the Home. One year the school children's collections reached one-fifth of the annual funds for the Home.

Thanksgiving Day Offerings

Ministers across the state were encouraged to designate their Thanksgiving Day Offering for the Home. Daddy Hall made suggestions for the churches fundraisers. Some were: a "loan exhibit" where the persons of the various nationalities displayed items from their cultures; a

A copy of "Children's Home Day" poster used in 1924.

"Harvest Home Festival" held the night before Thanksgiving with a speaker to tell about the Children's Home; and an old-fashioned basket social where persons could bid on baskets and socialize. All funds gathered were to be sent to the Home.

"Hazel Miner Circles"– Developed in 1921

During a severe snowstorm on March 15 and 16, 1920, Hazel Miner, the 16-year-old daughter of Mr. and Mrs. W. A. Miner of Center, North Dakota, gave her life heroically to save her brother and sister. Dismissed early from school due to the weather, the three children were in their one-horse sleigh. The horse dropped into a water hole and later the sleigh overturned. Hazel pulled canvas from the rig and placed the two young ones on the canvas. She covered her siblings with her coat and her body.

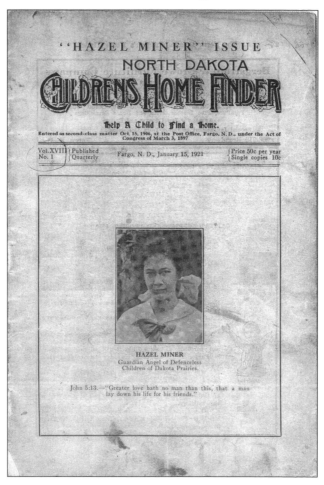

The Home We Shared

The next day when the blizzard subsided, they were found. She had saved the two younger children, but lost her own life.

With her saving spirit in mind, the Home began "Hazel Miner Circles" in her honor. The circles, usually made up of women, made plans for fundraisers or the construction of a new building that would save hundreds of needy children from hunger, cold, and homelessness. Not only did these circles meet monthly for fund raising, but they were instructed to watch for neglected and abused children in their own communities, who might need to be placed in the Home. Also, they were to watch over Society Wards placed in their communities.

Christmas "Red Stocking" Funds Used from 1926 to the Present Time

The "Red Stocking," another financial campaign, was started about the time that Daddy Hall became ill. The children made "Red Stockings" from construction paper. Following Thanksgiving, a stocking was enclosed in a letter, which told the needs of the Children's Home. They were mailed to people all across North Dakota. The toe of the stocking was formed into a pocket so it could be filled with a gift of money and returned to the Home. Through the Red Stocking Fund, persons were also encouraged to give gifts of blankets, food, toys, clothes, and books. All of these items were readily accepted by the workers at the Home and prepared as gifts to the children at Christmastime.

A New Home Was a Goal

Archives of the North Dakota Children's Home Society indicated that the goal of building a new Home was first raised in 1912. Below is the drawing of the future Home planned in 1924.

Proposed "Pioneers' Memorial Home for Dependent Children" on Watson Field, Fargo, N. D.

LAURA RUNDLE
As told by her granddaughter, Jan Hanson

Laura Rundle was born at Pinedale, Ontario, in 1871. She moved to LaRiviere, Monitoba, with her brother, who had an implement store there. Reverend Robeson of Hannah, North Dakota, then persuaded her to move to Hannah to play the church organ and give piano lessons. The following excerpt from a family history my cousin, Dave Bassingthwaite, is compiling, explains how she came to be at the North Dakota Children's Home.

"[Laura's] class was interrupted by a visit from an old friend from Ontario, who was superintendent of the Children's Home in Fargo. He was in need of a head nurse and had come to see if Reverend Robeson could help him find someone. Laura was not a nurse, but she was a four year college graduate and could substitute until a head nurse was found."

In 1902, while Laura was in Fargo, the "Hannah Moon" ran a story about her wanting to adopt Topsey, a little girl who lived at the Home. In the August, 1902, edition of the "North Dakota Children's Home Finder," Frank Hall writes about Topsey.

Laura Rundle

> This month the face of Topsey greets you on the first page. This bright little colored girl is the life of the Home, for there are heartaches shown here by those who give up children, that are not known outside such Homes. And the little black Topsey drives away such thoughts, for one look at her jolly face will bring a smile to anyone. Little does she know of the sorrows of her race, or of mankind in general, and less does she care. We could ill afford to lose Topsy, but unless her friends turn up pretty soon we shall have to find a home for her. Here is a chance for the genuine philanthropist to take this black little girl and give her a good home and a good chance to attend school.

The Home We Shared

Wedding photo of Laura and George Bassingthwaite

Laura didn't stay in Fargo long. She returned to Hannah (without Topsey) and went to the George Bassingthwaite farm to help take care of six children since his wife had just died in childbirth. Laura married him and they had six more children, five survived.

Author's Note

As I was researching for this book, I found an article on Topsey. No newspaper is mentioned, but it is possibly from the Fargo Argus, 1903. The writer uses language that never was acceptable terminology; but tells of great love for this child. Thus, I have decided to use it as written (see the following page.)

Found a Home at Last

Little Topsey, a Favorite Visitor to the Children's Home, is Dead

At the Children's Home on Friday night occurred the death of a little child who has become well known to visitors as "Topsey" — a little colored girl about 20 months old. "Topsey's" real name was Edna May Carmon, and she was placed in the Home for board by her mother, who came from Grand Forks more than a year ago. The mother paid her board for a few months, but since last spring nothing has been heard from her.

Superintendent Hall used every means to locate her, and finally, through a Methodist minister in Great Falls, Mont., got track of her grandmother; but no trace of the mother was ever discovered. After holding "Topsey" until December last that the mother might have every chance to provide for her, she was turned over to the Children's Home Society as a pauper child by the county commissioners for adoption. She was a source of great interest to all visitors to the Home, for she was a handsome pickaninny, full of fun, until a sickness last fall so reduced her strength that she scarcely smiled or moved. During the recent epidemic of measles at the Home she developed Bright's disease, which carried her off. A large number of friends attended the funeral service Sunday afternoon, which was conducted by Rev. E. W. Day.

Abandoned by her mother, "Topsey" was tenderly cared for at the Home and other hands than those of kith and kin laid beautiful flowers beside the little waif. Some people wonder why a fee is charged for the care of these waifs. There is a case where the society has been at an expense of more than $100 in caring for her; without the provision of a cent for expenses by anyone. Such cases run up the average cost greatly, and explain the requirement of a fee for; the expenses must be met in some way.

The society usually accepts between fifty and sixty children a year, and the cost of maintaining the work is about $5,000 per year. This makes the cost to the society for each child about $100 while the fee asked is $50, and even this is reduced in some cases or remitted altogether in especially worthy cases.

Every contribution to this cause helps care for some waif like "Topsey." She no longer needs a home, for her innocent little spirit is safe in those bright mansions above, but there are still others, who, like her, will always need some one to care for them. "Help a child to find a home."

Our Topsey

The Home We Shared

Dr. C.J. Dillon, M.D.
House Physician, February 1909-1939

In his annual reports to the Society Board, Dr. Dillon shared information about the children's illnesses, immunizations, surgeries, deaths, and he made recommendations. The following are excerpted from his notes.

April 1, 1914

Mortality; Nine deaths during the year from the following causes: Congenital heart trouble — one death, Acute Intestinal diarrhea — five deaths, Marasmus (inability to assimilate food) — three deaths. The youngest deceased was 45 days, the oldest deceased was 94 days. Average age among mortality 64-2/3 days.

Milk used in nursery is a bottled pasteurized cow's milk known as "Purity Brand" put on the market by Johnson Bros. of The Fargo Ice Cream and Dairy Co. We have used this milk for three years with perfect satisfaction and consider the Home fortunate that Fargo can boast of such an enterprising firm.

RECOMMENDATIONS: 1st, Playground and apparatus; 2nd, Enclosed porch; 3rd, Special Nursing in Acute Illness.

When an infant or child in the Home falls acutely ill, it is entitled to, and must receive, the same painstaking nursing and watchful care as the more fortunate child in the private home. In order to do this at times, it will be necessary to put a special nurse on the case, as usually the number of babies is enough to keep the regular force busily occupied. Our aim is to build up and perfect the system in the nursery, so that each helper will be capable of stepping up into the place of the one above them. Then the extra help that must be brought in, will easily fill the minor places.

April, 1915

The greatest affliction we have to contend with among our babies is a disease of nutrition called "inanition," which results either from improper feeding or lack of assimilation on the infant's part, and causes slow starvation. This inanition is very difficult to overcome in bottle-fed babies confined in crowded wards, and is responsible for the majority of deaths.

There is but one recommendation I wish to present to the Board for its consideration, and that is the utilization of the spacious grounds surrounding the Home as an attractive and well-equipped playground. Before we can fully discharge our obligations to our little charges, we must not only feed and clothe them, mother and father them, but we must also minister to their needs for wholesome play in attractive surroundings out-of-doors.

The Home We Shared

1926

A skating pond was made possible by flooding the lot at the corner of 11th Street. This work was done without charge by the City Department. Before Christmas, our children kept the pond cleared while the neighborhood skated. After Christmas, our children skated, as did also the staff. There was no room for any but our own. They all had a glorious time, and are so grateful.

January 1, 1936

<u>Accidents:</u> one Colle's fracture — a fall from the shed roof — Nesley Gandy. Anna Mae Frazier swallowed a locker key. Roy Snively lacerated hand and finger. Billy Bitz pushed a bead in the ear canal.

<u>Physical Examinations Made:</u> Forty-nine physical examinations were made as a new baby or child entered the Home. A routine complete chart or blank devised by the National Child Welfare League of America is filled out, giving a history of the individual, any ailments or physical handicaps, and recommendations for corrections and general care or management are written into the record.

<u>Isolation Cottage:</u> This additional facility (located on 8th Avenue to the East of the Home) has been a big factor in reducing the occurrence of illness and epidemics. Five groups of brothers and sisters numbering 19 in all were quartered in this isolation cottage at different times as they came to us. They are thus isolated for several weeks until we feel certain they are not bringing with them any communicable diseases such as head lice, the itch, measles, whooping cough, scarlet fever, etc.

1938

Modern preventive medicine and immunology have given the Home complete protection against small-pox and diphtheria and we might say almost complete protection against whooping cough and scarlet fever.

In February, there was a small epidemic of Chicken pox and in November a measles epidemic of 27 cases — nine of which were babies. By injecting these nine babies with blood taken from four of the old children convalescing from measles, the babies' attack was made much lighter, we believe. All 27 cases recovered.

An institution such as ours is bound to have more colds, more flu and such sickness due to crowded conditions. This is so in spite of good ventilation, proper hygiene, vitamins, cod liver oil and tonics. The organism causing common colds still is undetermined despite huge sums spent on the countless research laboratories by numerous research workers.

The Home We Shared

In 1939, Dr. Dillon had a severe stroke and died on March 17, 1941. He began as House Physician on February 18, 1909, and for 30 years had "given his time and skill that little children might have a better chance in life."

After 1939, many other doctors gave their medical service to the children at the Home. A few were: Dr. Ralph Pray, Dr. Lancaster, Dr. William Armstrong, and Dr. Bernard Mazure.

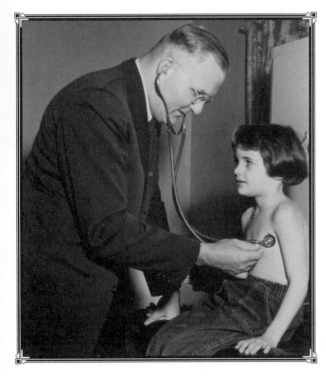

Dr. Bernard Mazure and a child.

The Home We Shared

Lucy J. (Babcock) Hall

One experience I missed while growing up at the Home was traveling by buggy, train, or car with Lucy Hall, the daughter-in-law of Frank "Daddy" Hall. Literally thousands of North Dakota children would have had that privilege, although due to the circumstances of that moment, they might not have felt very privileged. The children would not realize the magnitude of the personality with whom they were traveling. Neither would they understand the great thought behind the decision to relieve them from parents and their present living conditions, nor the reasons for the new relationships they would soon be forming through foster care and adoption.

It would be interesting to hear one of the "Lucy and child" conversations. Most were probably overwhelmed by the new landscapes as they moved across the state. Lucy's small frame, not much larger than most 12 year olds, was nonthreatening to the children, and most likely the children felt free to ask questions, "Why am I leaving my parents?" or "What will my new family be like?" I'm quite sure that Lucy, with her reassuring countenance, answered each and every question in her moderate, calm voice.

For a span of 42 years, 1912 to 1954, Lucy Hall assisted with the personal care or placement of over 6,000 children at the Home. From 1929 to 1936, she was temporarily assigned to District Judge, George A. McKenna and William H. Hutchinson for the sole purpose of establishing a juvenile commission office in North Dakota's third judicial district. During those years, she continued to work part-time for the Home.

At her retirement in 1954, Lucy Hall referred to her good driving record with great pride. Over all the years in her position of caseworker, she had "no accidents." Usually, she would drive over a thousand miles per week.

Lucy's first travels were by horse and buggy or train. Next, she learned to drive a Model T with hand-worked windshield wipers and speeds of 20 miles per hour. Then, she "graduated" to her Model A and it could obtain speeds of 40 miles per hour. We must not forget that on these travels, usually at least one child would be seated nearby her or a whole family using all the seats. What a responsibility for this woman!

Lucy was born on August 14, 1888 in Fargo, N.D. to Mr. S.B. and Mrs. "Mittie" Babcock. She graduated from Fargo High School and Fargo College. In 1908, she married Jeremiah Lawrence Hall, son of Frank Drew and Nellie Hart Hall. It was a shock when her husband of less than one year died suddenly of pneumonia in April of 1909. Just a few weeks later, Lucy gave birth at the Hall home to their son and named him "Lawrence Babcock Hall."

After his son's death, Daddy Hall decided to homestead in Golden Valley on the Little Missouri River. The homestead was located in the Northern Dakota Badlands, near Teddy Roosevelt's ranch. Frank and

The Home We Shared

Nellie, along with their adopted daughter, Clara, moved to their homestead and set up housekeeping in a house with one room and an attic. To get there, the Halls traveled by stage to Wibaux, Montana, then by horse and buggy or bobsled the remaining 30 miles to their house. Frank stayed only one month, before returning to his work at the Home, leaving Nellie and Clara there alone.

When Frank and Nellie's son, Donald, was out of school for the summer, he traveled with Lucy and her son, Lawrence, out west to join Nellie and Clara on the homestead. Frank thought it would be good for all of them to have a "real pioneering in the wild country experience."

In 1910, Clara injured her back; thus the family had to return to Fargo at Christmastime to seek medical attention. By the time of Donald's graduation from Fargo High School in 1913, the pioneering spirit had been forgotten, as all focused on their work and studies in Fargo.

Group of Children's Home Nurses. Back row: Miss Emma Nordboe, and Mrs. Lucy Hall. Front row: Mrs. Hohn Cooke, Matron Carey, and Mrs. Cora Bennett.

When little Lawrence reached school age in 1912, Lucy Hall became the head nurse for the Children's Home. Two years later, Dr. J.G. Dillon, the Home doctor, requested that Lucy get an increase in salary. He sent a note to the Society's Nov. 5, 1914, board meeting, asking that "Miss" Lucy Hall's salary be raised from $30 per month to $50 per month. Board meeting minutes indicate that the suggestion was deferred to a future meeting.

In the years to follow, Lucy took on various responsibilities, as an office worker, matron, caseworker, and finally casework supervisor. On the days she was in the Home office, I remember seeing her at her desk typing or using the phone. Once I learned to type, I was given permission to use her typewriter during the evening hours to prepare my term papers for college.

Often I assisted my mother, Mary, in preparing a baby to be "shown" to a couple for adoption. The exchange of the child occurred in the large foyer or Lucy's office. Then, Lucy Hall would take the child into the Library so the parents-to-be could make their decision behind closed doors. Lucy was very careful to place children in homes that fit their character and background.

Lucy's pioneer spirit, picked up when living at the Hall's homestead in the western part of the state, never left her. She enjoyed being outdoors as often as possible. Each spring Lucy gathered a group of families, mine included, at Tourist Park for the first picnic of the season. We were always the first in the spring and the last in the fall to picnic in the park — in the fall this meant sitting near the campfire to stay warm. These same families gathered throughout the year to celebrate each of

Lucy Hall, 1948.

their birthdays.

Each summer, Lucy traveled at least once a month to Camp Watson. Because there was no phone at the camp, it was her car turning into the gate that started a ripple through the camp participants wondering, "Is she bringing a new child to camp?" or "Who will be leaving?" Often the excuse given for a child's leaving was, "He/she needs her tonsils out." I wonder to this day, if they all actually did have their tonsils removed before they went into foster care or were adopted.

While at camp, Lucy swam a

Lucy Hall and Dorothy Lund, 1939.

The Home We Shared

number of times each day. She often stayed one or two days and overnight(s) — a short "vacation" for this hard-working woman.

Lucy was always proud of her son, Lawrence. He graduated from Fargo Central High School in 1928, and the North Dakota Agricultural College in 1936. He went on to receive his Master's degree from Oregon State in mechanical engineering. During World War II, Lawrence was assigned to Burma as a Malaria Control Sanitation Engineer. One day, Lucy received a letter from him describing the harrowing experience of fleeing from Burma through China to New Delhi, India.

On June 24th, 1954, Lucy retired from the North Dakota Children's Home Society. Lawrence and his daughter, Peggy, came from Georgia to attend the retirement party, as well as many people from all across North Dakota.

To honor Lucy Hall for her many years of service, the board of directors of the Home adopted the following resolution.

> Whereas: Lucy J. Hall, for 42 years, from May 8, 1912, to July 1, 1954, served the North Dakota Children's Home Society devotedly and tirelessly, and;
>
> Whereas: She, as a planner of the destiny of thousands of children, with all of its detailed work and uncountable problems, never lost sight of the real objective — the most happiness, security, love and protection possible for each child — and that each child be counted as an individual with rights and feelings and desires and ambitions; and that she distinguished herself and the Society on numerous occasions through her efforts in the area of child welfare work in North Dakota; and that she sacrificed continually her personal time and financial gain so that homeless and dependent children might find greater happiness, and;
>
> Whereas: She served, through the Society, over six thousand children while traveling nearly one half million miles in the performance of her duties.
>
> NOW THEREFORE BE IT RESOLVED, that we, the officers and Board of Directors, extend to Lucy Hall our sincere thanks and great appreciation for the outstanding service to children so freely given over and above the normal call of duty, and we wish her all happiness in the days to come, and will be grateful to her, not only for what she has always done but for what we know she will continue to do for children's welfare.
>
> This is to certify that the above resolution was unanimously adopted on May 6, 1954, by the vote of the undersigned officer and directors of the North Dakota Children's Home Society.

THE HOME WE SHARED

HAROLD H. BOND
OUR "FATHER FIGURE," JULY, 1927–MAY, 1951

When Frank Hall suffered his unexpected and disabling stroke in 1926, he had served the Society and Home for 24 years. The Board placed Miss Margaret MacGunigal, the Director of the Children's Bureau of North Dakota, as the Acting Superintendent. Miss Jean Love, a field worker for the Home, became the Secretary. Then, the Board went out to seek a new leader.

In 1927, they hired Harold H. Bond, the Superintendent of Schools from Slope County, North Dakota, as new Superintendent for the Home. Mr. Bond and his wife, Brownie, moved in just across the alley, east of the Home. Regardless of the hour or day, they were always available to meet the needs of the children and staff.

Harold Bond was a most gentle and giving person and the children felt his love and concern as his tall lanky figure moved quietly among the children. He and Brownie had dinner parties for a few of the children in their home. They were always ready to celebrate holidays and birthdays, adding fun to the children's lives.

In 1935, Mr. Bond began dreaming of a "new, modern, multi-building place for the children." It wasn't until after his retirement in 1951 that the dream came to fruition. Before opening the new facility in 1956, the board of directors decided to rename the three-building village, "Children's Village," so the general public would understand that the funding was through personal and private gifts, not from the state of North Dakota.

The following insights, written by Mr. Bond, are taken from the Society's annual board minutes.

1930 Annual Report

Your Society is asked to assist in so many ways; in every case, there is a child to be considered. The Society is called upon to help iron out family difficulties; provide boarding-care for children; accept children committed to it by the district courts of the state; find a home for the child left without parents or proper guardian; and to help provide and arrange hospital care and treatment for

Mr. Harold H. bond, circa late 1930s.

sick or crippled children. All requests, of whatever nature, could be summed up in one sentence or request; "This child, thru no fault of his own, is not having a square deal. Will you take him and give him his chance in life?"

Your children in the Receiving Home have enjoyed good health due to the daily visits of Dr. Dillon and the splendid assistance of the staff of doctors and nurses at both the Fargo and the Dakota Clinics. Some of your children have had to be cared for at St. John's and St. Luke's Hospitals, and the staff at each place seem to take a special interest in these children. Drs. Ewy, Sand, and Leonard have given of their time and service to care for the children's teeth; Drs. Knudson and Winn can be counted on at any time for treatment of any eye, ear, or throat trouble.

The Mayo Clinic at Rochester, Minnesota, took care of four operative cases during the year, and we appreciate more than we can tell, the interest shown children from this Society by the Medical Social Service of the Mayo Clinic.

1931 Annual Report

Each year this report attempts to bring to you something of the personal service in every day of the year. Miss Love and Miss Wells, your caseworkers, have traveled over forty thousand miles the past year and have interviewed thousands of people in their efforts to help these children who ask for assistance. Day or night, good roads and bad, they have covered the entire state several times. They are happy over a piece of work well done, another child made comfortable, another good home found. Your house staff, those charged with the care of the children, continues to give untiring effort. Every child is important and precious in their (the worker's) eyes; they strive to have all the children in the best physical condition possible.

June 21, 1932, Children's Home workers and children celebrating the 32nd anniversary of the Home.

Miss Laybourne and Mr. Bond with Hansie's Fancy Cakes! June 21, 1932

1932 Home workers — Back row: Emma Gray, laundress; Mrs. Raines; Amil Lund; Jean Love; and Harold Bond. Front row: Esther Hartrickson; "Pat"Wells; "Brownie" Bond; Henrietta Hanson, cook; Selma Kruger; Mary Lund; and Mabel Miller.

At a time when all Railroads are looking ahead, trying to see just what the future holds for them, we are so grateful for their willingness to do their share. Never have the Northern Pacific, the Great Northern, the Milwaukee, or the Great Western refused our request for transportation for any of your wards or for any member of the Society traveling in the interest of some dependent child.

All of your children of school age, who reside at the Receiving Home for even a short time, attend the public schools of Fargo. We wish to call attention to the fact that the school board of the Fargo Public Schools has been most considerate in handling this problem. It is not an easy matter to arrange. Children come and go, change schools, are in and out; but, always, principals and teachers and the school board have cheerfully complied with our requests, and to them all and to the City of Fargo are due a good share of any success that we may have had the past year."

1932 Annual Report

At times, we have needed to ask for special study and observation of children who are mentally retarded and we acknowledge the fine help given us by Dr. A.R.T. Wylie of the Institution for Feeble-Minded at Grafton, and by Dr. Humpstone of the University of North Dakota.

Receipts were smaller, but our service to children did not suffer. Miss Jean Love and Miss Elizabeth Wells, field workers, have given good faithful service. An idea of their activities can be had when you know they traveled over 30,000 miles in the interests of children. They made more than 320 supervision visits, wrote 292 supervisory letters, made 94 home investigations, transferred 55 children, worked on 153 Special Aid cases.

A total of over 2,000 interviews were held.

1935 Annual Report

Our office and field force has been inadequate to meet the needs since the resignation of Miss Jean Love. But, will again function as before when Mrs. Lucy J. Hall, known to all members of the Society, takes her place as case-supervisor and assistant to the Superintendent on March 1st, 1936.

It would not do to close this report without reference to our ever present need — Suitable Housing for Children and Staff. Present quarters are not satisfactory in that the Receiving Home cannot meet the demands made upon it. How much longer we can continue to use the present building is a guess, as each year sees greater repair bills, and we have definite hazards that cannot be overlooked. The answer is to build four to five smaller units to house selected groups of children, each in the charge of a housemother. This would take the place of the Receiving Home and would do away with all housing problems. The cost would not be great. Your Superintendent has an idea that this will appeal to some person soon who, in memory of some dear one and to sweeten the lives of little unfortunate children, will erect the first unit in our plan. (His dream was fulfilled 20 years later in 1956 when "Children's Village" opened on South University Drive, Fargo, North Dakota.)

1939 Annual Report

Cut in expenses had to be made somewhere to meet the 18 percent cut in our state appropriation. Expense of food and clothing and service to children must go on, so this emergency was met when each member of the office and house staff agreed to do without salary for one month in order that these children in our care might not suffer.

1940 Annual Report

1940 was a year filled with activity, and, we believe a year of good service to children in need. As in other years the Society was called upon to give many kinds of service. We recall all of the following types of cases:
- Care of babies and their placement or return to mothers,
- Care of small boys and girls removed from their homes because of bad or cruel treatment by parents,
- Care and plans for older boys and girls on the edge of delinquency,
- Care and planning for many crippled children under the State program,
- Care and return of runaway children from other states,
- Special medical treatments for certain children,
- Investigation of cases reported by Juvenile Courts,
- Investigation of foster and boarding homes,
- Working with other states in plans for North Dakota children,
- Special studies of certain children who were misfits in their own homes,
- Preparing of Juvenile Court cases to be heard.

1941 Annual Report — The War

A World War affects everybody. Your Society is feeling the natural results where all-out efforts are directed toward greater output of war material and manpower. People who have relatives in our armed forces; people who are doing all they can to purchase War Bonds and Stamps; people who are meeting increased living costs and double income tax payments, cannot be expected to contribute to Social Work as they have in the past.

The Society is being of direct help to many former wards of the Society in securing birth records. A large number of these would be unable to secure birth certificates without the assistance of your Society. Our records are the only ones available and we are happy to give this service even tho it takes much of our time each day. We hear from Sailors, Soldiers, Flyers, and Marines; former wards who are now doing their part in the struggle for decent living. It is good to know that your Society had something to do with building up these characters; every one an enlisted man so far, who think it worthwhile to fight and die for the form of government under which we live.

1942 is (will be) a war year and we cannot know what demands may be made upon your Society for the care of children. We are making plans whereby we may be ready to serve the needs of the State and the Country if some emergency should arise.

The Home We Shared

1942 Annual Report

The face sheet of this report is a reminder that many of the wards of your Society are in active service in this Great War. There are many others than are listed and we have used the names of those with whom we are in touch. They have had many experiences and so far all are safe. One has traveled the western seas for two years, fought in three sea battles and endured the bombs of Pearl Harbor. Another has had two ships sunk from under him and, not satisfied with the share he has contributed, will soon fly navy planes in combat. It is interesting to note that these are farm boys of North Dakota. We are with each one of these lads in spirit and prayer.

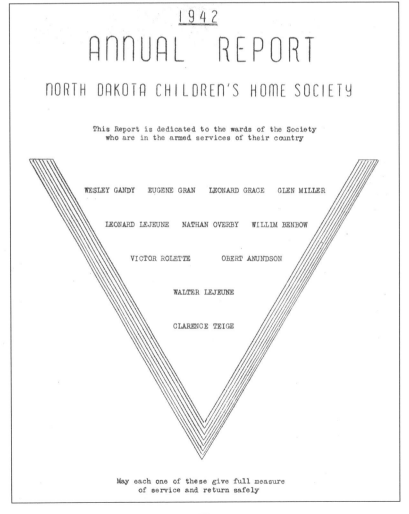

1942
ANNUAL REPORT
NORTH DAKOTA CHILDREN'S HOME SOCIETY

This Report is dedicated to the wards of the Society who are in the armed services of their country

WESLEY GANDY   EUGENE GRAN   LEONARD GRACE   GLEN MILLER

LEONARD LEJEUNE   NATHAN OVERBY   WILLIM BENBOW

VICTOR ROLETTE   OBERT ANUNDSON

WALTER LEJEUNE

CLARENCE TEIGE

May each one of these give full measure of service and return safely

The Home We Shared

Maintaining a house staff is always a problem and there have been some changes. Mr. Lund, feeling that he was needed in more essential war work, went to work for Henry Kaiser building ships near Portland, Oregon. For two months your Superintendent did double duty. This problem was solved when Mr. Lund returned the first of the year. Mr. and Mrs. Lund are very important people in the plan of your Society and we must do all we can to keep them happy and satisfied. Some better living quarters must be provided in the Receiving Home for them. This is our great need.

We owe much to Mrs. Lucy J. Hall, Case Supervisor, who for many years has done so much to help hundreds of unhappy, homeless children into good foster homes and a happy life. With her own son very ill in India, Mrs. Hall has carried on with a fine spirit and her services are much appreciated.

1943 will be an interesting year. We have faith in our Government. We have faith in our armed forces and have no doubt of victory and a lasting peace. We close with a thought — "Children are Priority Number 1, don't forget them this next year."

The Home in the 1950s emptied out for Crippled Children's Program.

1943 Special Meeting of Executive Committee; Tuesday, Sept. 14th

Under a slightly new plan of operation of the Receiving Home, and in order to get more efficient work and to properly allot the many duties, Mr. Lund was appointed House Manager with full control of the Receiving Home and authority to look out for the children, etc. Mrs. Lund was named House Mother and will have complete charge of the house staff, the children, all feeding and clothing for the children and the

The Home We Shared

purchasing of such food, clothing, etc, as may be necessary. They are both fulltime every day and will have a combined salary of $200.00 (per month) with maintenance.

(The Budget included an improvements list and costs for a 10'x12' room to be added on to the Lund's one-room apartment at the cost of $850.00. An outside entrance and porch we added, too.)

Mr. Bond further explained that the roof of the proposed new room would also serve as the floor for a porch to be used for a sunroom for the babies in the nursery. A door will be cut thru from the nursery to permit the cribs to be wheeled out on this porch. (The porch was never constructed.)

Board of Directors Meeting; June 1, 1944

Mr. Bond spoke of the two former wards of the Society who had met death in the armed service of their country, William Benbow and Leonard Grace.

Those present were taken out to see the addition made to the quarters of Mr. and Mrs. Lund and they were pleased with what had been done.

President (E.G.) Clapp expressed his appreciation and that of all the members of the Board of Directors - to the contributions made by each member of the Staff — each helper in the home, to Mr. and Mrs. Lund in particular, to Mrs. Lucy J. Hall for her many years of helpful service and to Mr. and Mrs. Bond.

A rear view of the Home showing the built-on room for Myra and Dorothy.

1945 Annual Report

Children attended public schools as usual and the Sunday schools of their choice. They took part in the school programs and games and felt themselves a part of the community, just as much as those who lived here all their lives. All the older boys and girls spent two and one-half months at our fine Cottage at Pelican Lake in the summer. This was a wonderful opportunity to have them outdoors most of the time and in the water several times every day.

Last year the Society disposed of the North 12 lots of the 13th Street property (at 13th Avenue) and will try to sell the remaining 14 lots when a buyer can be found. Selling this property commits the Society to make use of the 10th Street lots where our present buildings stand. This is as it should be and it is just suited to our use. Before very long we hope to build two or three houses on this property. Each would have a housemother and care for 8 – 10 children. This plan is a good one and much better than one building where children of all ages and both sexes are housed together. We hope this dream will come true before too long as it is a first need.

1946 Annual Report — a successful year

In the area of placement for adoption the report shows that during 1946 the Society received a total of 97 formal applications from individuals wishing to adopt children. Of this 97, 85 were from persons who had not previously taken a child and 12 were from persons who had previously taken one child and wished a second child. In addition to the formal applications for a child, there were 51 informal inquiries from persons interested. During the year the members of the receiving home staff investigated a total of 45 prospective adoptive homes, of which 42 were approved, and three were disapproved. Supervisory visits made during the year totaled 226.

Brownie and Harold H. Bond, 1946.

The Home We Shared

Mr. Bond with the younger children in the children's dining room, 1948.

Mr. Bond with children on the "playground," 1948.

The Home We Shared

1949, December – "Christmas Stocking" Letter

A copy of Mr. Bond's last "Christmas Stocking" letter brings his historical record to a close. The letter was mailed to the general public in 1949 and included a paper cut out of a stocking. Persons were to fill the toe with their gift and return the stocking.

This great personality would retire the following year; but he was asked to remain through 1951 to assist with the financial part of the Home as they were preparing to develop the "Children's Village" on South University Drive, across from the Dakota Hospital. Soon "the dreams" of "Daddy Hall" and Harold Bond would be realized.

North Dakota Children's Home Society
804 TENTH STREET SOUTH
Fargo, North Dakota

"Merry Christmas"

December, 1949

Dear Children of our Sunday Schools:

Here it is getting close to Christmas and many of our children wonder what it will mean for them. Not that they won't get Christmas gifts, for they always do, but they are wondering whether they will have a home to live in by then. You see, most of them do not have a mother or a father to care for them.

We of the North Dakota Children's Home Society can supply the food, clothing and medical care that these children need, and we can also find good homes for each one, but not unless you help us. If you children could think of a way to raise a little money and send it to us in the enclosed Christmas Stocking, it would mean that all these things could be done for our homeless children. Your Sunday School Superintendent will help you work out a way to do this.

We have 43 children here with us now, 12 of them little babies. All of them, yes the babies too, send greetings and a Merry Christmas to each one of you.

Sincerely yours,

Harold H. Bond
Superintendent

THE HOME WE SHARED

ROBERT C. OLSLUND
SUPERINTENDENT FROM 1950-1957

With the resignation of Harold H. Bond, the Society Board selected a 26-year-old man, Robert Olslund, to take on the responsibilities of not only managing the Home, staff, and children; but also, developing "the dreams" of a new place — the dreams placed before the Board in 1920, over 30 years ago.

Olslund was a graduate of Fargo Central High School in 1942. He attended North Dakota Agricultural College (NDAC) and was in ROTC. His classes were interrupted when he joined the Naval Air Corps. After 16 months of training, Olslund flew F6 Hellcats Navy Fighters from a carrier in the Atlantic Ocean just as World War II ended.

When he accepted the position of Superintendent of the Children's Home, Olslund had no idea the intensity of the task before him. The Home was facing changing times at the end of the war. Robert and the staff would not just be taking care of the feeding, clothing, and educating of the children. Now, there were many emotional disorders and many of the children arrived as "delinquents."

Robert recalls many hours spent in the courtrooms trying to take care of the needs of these youth. The Cass County Welfare Board became more involved as they started a Children's Social Services division and

Mrs. G.A. Fraser, who served as a member of the Women's Boarding Home Association in Fargo for 40 years, handed a check for $22,762 to G.W. Jensen, treasurer of the North Dakota Children's Home in Fargo. Present for the transaction, which marked the end of the association, are (left to right): Mrs. B.G. Rose, president; Mrs. Lloyd Krieg, secretary; Mrs. Fraser; Mrs. Stanley Gelder, treasurer; Jensen; Milton F. Weber, member of the executive committee of the children's home, and Robert Olslund, superintendent of the children's home. (Fargo Forum photo, November 15, 1953).

had staff psychologists available to these youth.

Mr. Olslund and his wife, Eleanore, were raising three children in their own home; but many nights' sleep were interrupted by the phone calls from the police asking his assistance with neglected children who had been left alone by their parents. Robert became the "buffer", as most of the children were afraid of the policemen. He remembers sitting beside the frightened children and explaining where he and the police would be taking them, until their parents were found.

Some of the neglected children stayed only six to eight weeks at the Home while their parents went through the court system. Others became "wards of the state" and were available for adoption.

He remembers the busy summers with the Crippled Children's Program, the many hours transporting the patients to and from the hospitals for surgery and to the clinics for their treatments. Part of his evening schedule was to assist with carrying the children to their bedrooms on second floor and each morning to carry them down for meals and scheduled treatments.

Because fulfilling "The Dream" of a new home or cottages was the most important item on the Board's list, Olslund was seeking information about existing homes throughout the Midwest. He and Children's Home board member, Milton F. Weber, traveled many miles to view Children's Homes. He remembers going to "Boy's Town" in Omaha, Nebraska. They visited homes in Minnesota and at Chicago, Illinois. They took the best of each existing home and soon the plans began to form.

Two large financial gifts helped Olslund lead the Board into a final decision to begin the buildings. Mr. Frederick Reynolds had died in California, leaving an estate of $388,000.00 to the Society. This would be paid in yearly installments of $120,000.

Then, the Women's Boarding Home Association closed their "Robert's Hill Hall for Women," located at 120 8th Street South, which had served as a rooming house for young, out-of-town girls, who wanted to attend Fargo Central High School. When it closed in the fall of 1953, the Home was given a check for $22,762.00.

In 1955, an architect and a contractor were hired and the three cottages that made up "Children's Village" were built. Children's Village opened in 1956.

Having achieved "The Dream," Robert resigned in 1957 to go into business of his own. He, his wife, and sons own the Hintz Fire Equipment, Inc. store on Main and 15th Street So in Fargo.

In 2004, his sons run the business and he and Eleanore have enjoyed many years of retirement. He continues to have fond memories of the years he supervised the Home. The many children's faces cross his mind and he tells of the good work done by the staff.

The Home We Shared

Mabel Miller
By Jennifer Radack
From the Centennial Edition of "The Village Crier"
Vol. 19, No.1 – November 1991

The year was 1932; America was suffocating under a thick blanket of economic depression. Mabel Miller, age twenty-two, could be found sleeping outside in the shaded grass, trying to avoid the oppressive heat of the small four room cottage she shared with two others. She usually tried to sleep in the morning, since she worked all night as a nurse at the Children's Home.

Graduating from college, one of the few opportunities waiting for Mabel was at the Home. "It was very poor pay, but I really needed the money. I only made a half of what the girls before me made. Yet, there weren't many jobs to choose from, and the Home gave free room and board."

The hardest part of the job for Mabel was the infringement on her social life. "I was only twenty-two, and had to work seven nights a week. I had Sundays off, which meant I didn't have to report to work until ten o'clock that night." But the joys of the job were many. "I'm glad I had the experience, it was wonderful. I can still see the smiles on those little guys' faces."

Mabel's evenings started at six o'clock when she began folding diapers — many stacks reaching waist high. At seven o'clock she began feeding the babies, recalling that there was always at least five, and at times the number of babies in the nursery reached eighteen

Mabel Miller was a nruse at the Children's Home in the 1930s.

or twenty. "I'd sing to them, and rock them. I'd take turns with them, one in each arm. I just loved singing to those little babies."

Mabel remembers a grandfather coming to the Home early one morning to drop off a newborn. He had driven all night, after finding the child's mother trying to suffocate her. "That one came in without a name. She was a lovely baby. Esther Hartvikson, the other nurse, and I, named her Noendes. It was a name out of a story we had read."

Mabel loved the babies like they were her own. She slowly turns the tattered pages of an old photo album. "People always asked me why I didn't adopt one. I could have had them all, any one of them." She points to a photograph of her younger self, holding a beautiful baby girl. "This one was with us for about a year when the mother's father brought her to see the baby. She was very young, and her mother wouldn't acknowledge that there even was a baby. She came that day and signed her away. She was a very pretty girl, her baby looked just like her. She took this picture here, of me holding her daughter."

Mabel recalled, "A heartbreaking part of working in the nursery was not knowing when the babies were going to leave. Some nights when I came to work, one baby would be gone. It was always a surprise. I felt just like someone had died."

There were also many sad situations that Mabel had to deal with. One night, some time after midnight, Mr. Bond (housefather and superintendent at that time) brought a young brother and sister to Mabel. He told me to give them baths and put them to bed. They were both shaking and scared. When I put the little boy to bed, his sister began to cry and tell me she wanted to be with him. I tucked her in and told her she'd see her brother first thing in the morning, at breakfast." Mabel never found out where Mr. Bond had found them, or what happened to them. She just kept her place and gave them all the love she could give while they stayed.

After five years of the night shift, Mabel had simply worn herself out. "I was losing weight, and my right kidney had slipped out of place from too much lifting. I was also married by this time, and felt I needed a life of my own." So Mabel left the Home, taking a lifetime of rewarding memories with her. As she closes the photo album, she sums up the best part of working there with a peaceful smile. "Just loving the kids, that was the best part."

The Home We Shared

Remembering Some of the Other Workers

Esther Hartvickson

Miss Esther Hartvickson was a very slender, tall woman who was the "Day Nurse." She was born in Nomdalen, Norway on September 28, 1899 and was Naturalized in 1915. There is no record as to when she began working in the Nurseries at the Home; but, photos show her there in the late 20's. She continued working until the Home moved to the new buildings.

Miss Hartvickson lived in a room with a bath on the second floor. Her apartment was over the front door. She worked long hours during each day. She ate her meals in the Staff Dining room and usually was buried behind the morning newspaper, "The Christian Science Monitor," and in the evenings, "The Fargo Forum." She was usually quiet and kept to herself.

Mrs. Laybourne was a beautiful, loving woman who lived across the street in the apartments. Because she lived so near her work, she was there every day to take care of the children. She would wake the children, see that they got dressed, ring the bell for meals and serve their breakfast.

Mrs. Laybourne would see the children off to school and back at noon for their next meal, then, off to school for the afternoon. The younger children would take their naps. She would await the older ones to return from school. She served the evening meal and encouraged the study times, then, all off to bed. Then, she could return to her home. This wonderful woman gave her life to these children. For some reason, there is no individual photo of her.

Miss Raines. The children speak of Miss Raines' red hair and her kindness.

"Hansie," the cook made fabulous meals! She never complained and worked well with the teenagers assigned to assist in the kitchen and with clean up. She had a great talent for decorating cakes for birthdays and holidays. My recollection is that she resigned after she met and married Max, and they settled down in their new home.

"Hansie," the cook.

Miss Graffee was a large, peppy person, who came to the USA during World War II. I think she was Jewish and had escaped from Germany where she had worked with children, also. She was active in B'NAI B'rith and taught Esperanto in the community. Miss Graffee loved children and led Camp Fire Girls on her time off.

Miss Gray was a tall, thin woman who worked for years in the laundry. It seemed to be the best place for her, as she was self-conscious of her speech problem. She worked long hours in this dark, damp, hot place.

Mr. and Mrs. Peter Waldera were hired just before the Home moved to the Children's Village.

All the Other Workers, who I have not named. The children loved each worker, who gave unselfishly to make life the best for the children at the Home.

Mrs. Peter Waldera with the children.

Peter Waldera, 1950s.

Workers Edna, Kennedy, John, Graffee Hartvickson, 1945.

The Home We Shared

Mathilda Decker, Mabel Miller, and Esther Hartvickson, 1930s.

Brownie Bond, Dorothy and Harold H. Bond, 1938.

Miss Mathilda Decker.

Harold H. Bond and Amil J. Lund, meet in California, 1964.

The Home We Shared

The Barber's College come to give hair cuts, 1952.

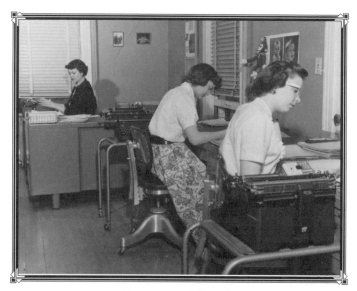

Home office staff, 1952.

Brownie Bond and the mailman.

Hansie.

Miss Graffee.

Amil and Mary Lund's 25th wedding anniversary party, 1955. "People who were at their wedding." Back row: Lucy Hall, Esther Hartvickson, Mr. & Mrs. Bill McGrath. Front row: Eloise Leazer Johnson, Amil and Mary.

The Home We Shared

THE HOME WE SHARED

OUR SHARED PARENTS
1926-1955

MARY ALBERNA LEAZER LUND
AMIL JUSTINE LUND

THE HOME WE SHARED

MARY ALBERNA LEAZER LUND

Mary Leazer (my mother) took a final, slow look about the spacious bedroom she shared with her three sisters. Numerous parsonages across Minnesota and Iowa had been home to her. This one was located in Morningside near the larger community of Sioux City, Iowa, and was the place where the Leazer family had resided for the longest time, eight years. To leave her home and family members was an emotional event.

The Leazer Family: Eva, 19; Katie, 18; Alfred, 17; Clarence, 16; Leon, 13; George, 10; Mary, 9; Florence, 7; Helen, 5; Lucille, 2. August 5, 1907.

Mary's departure would not only be a physically closing of a door at her home; but also, a closing to an unusual style of living as the "preacher's kid." This life involved sessions of memorizing the Psalms, learning hymns in four-part harmony, and searching for the right outfit from the Mission Barrel. The congregation gathered clothes to be sent to the mission field; but the preacher's family was allowed to select outfits before the barrels were sealed and shipped.

It was time for her to venture from her parents and four siblings who remained at home and head out to continue her education. Five siblings had already left home on their journeys; one each to New Mexico, Nebraska and California, the other two to Chili and Peru, South America. Mary's destination was Sioux City, only a few miles away.

After Mary had graduated from Morningside High School, she, like seven of her siblings, took classes at Morningside College, an institution sponsored by the Methodist denomination. Now she had selected a

The Home We Shared

career in nursing, and was moving into an apartment near the Maternity Hospital in Sioux City, where she would attend school.

Slipping out the bedroom door and moving along the hallway, she approached the winding staircase. Descending, Mary's pace slowed until she paused on the bottom step. She felt uneasy leaving her father and mother, the Reverend Fred and Ida May (Lindsay) Leazer as they had been aging so quickly these past few years. Taking the last step, she walked toward the vestibule. There, she gathered her parents close to her and embraced each of them. She could return every few weeks to visit with them, but now, she must be off to complete her nurse's training. She walked confidently out the front door and waved back to her dear parents.

Mary enjoyed the apartment and the two young women nursing students who shared it with her. The Maternity Hospital allowed for a good learning experience led by her adept instructors. Since the school was located within a hospital, Mary had many opportunities to be involved at the time of births. She also worked in the nursery with the infants and at the bedside of the recovering mothers.

In 1919, she graduated from the Sioux City Maternity Hospital as a certified midwife. Now, she was constantly on call to assist area women with the birthing process. After the baby arrived, she stayed in their home, as long as a month, taking care of the mother, the newborn, and any older children. When the mother was strong enough to take on her household responsibilities, Mary moved on to assist another family.

As additional children were born, she often made repeat visits to the same families. Mary's presence was so greatly appreciated that she was considered "family" and invited to their gatherings in the years that followed.

Mary Leazer's graduation, 1919.

Also, Mary was called to help the Leazer family and relatives. She "nursed" many of the children through various illnesses, such as Measles, Chicken Pox, and Whooping Cough.

In 1923, Mary grieved the death of her father, Fred E. Leazer. He had heart failure and died on December 4th before medical assistance could arrive. On the day of her father's funeral, a niece died from Whooping

Cough. These were lonely days for Mary and her mother. The next year Mary experienced another shock when her mother, Ida May, died on June 10th, just seven months after her husband's death, of old age and a broken heart.

Mary continued her work as a midwife and assisted her siblings and their families. Often, she was the person selected to take her sisters to their new jobs or on tours of the country "in her Mary automobile." They had great times traveling and camping, even taking in the views at the Royal Gorge and driving to the top of Pikes Peak in Colorado.

During the early part of 1926, Mary received a letter from Dr. Dillon, house physician at the North Dakota Children's Home in Fargo, North Dakota. He asked her to move to Fargo to become the "Receiving Home Matron."

He went on to describe the Home and her job; it all sounded so interesting. The Newborn Nursery could hold up to eight babies, the Toddler Nursery could accommodate twenty toddlers! The care of all of these little ones would be her responsibility. Another part of her job would be to assist in making decisions concerning the health needs of the older children. For all ages of children, other workers would assist her.

Not only would she have a salary, but also, would receive "room and board," a small, unfurnished bedroom with a bath in the Home, and all her meals in the staff dining room.

Mary's room at the Home.

Mary Leazer.

Mary accepted the new position and prepared to leave for North Dakota in May of 1926. She packed her small writing desk and dressing table with the three-fold mirror with bench to match. She placed her clothes in a large cedar chest and a leather trunk, and sent them ahead to Fargo by train.

When the day came for her to begin her 350-mile journey to the Home, Mary adjusted her flapper-style dress and placed her felt hat on her head. Then, she picked up, in one hand, her satchel that held her clothing for the trip. In the other hand, she carried the brown leather medical bag that contained all the supplies she needed for health emergencies.

It was time to leave. With certainty, she walked to her newly purchased car, a Whippet, and drove off to start a great adventure and enjoy the new opportunity!

Mary's Whippet. Mary Leazer and Mattie Morgan — old friends meet again in Fargo.

Amil Justine Lund

The year was 1908. Amil Justine Lund (my father) was only five years old as he watched his parents, Oscar and Betsy (Dahl) Lund, pack up their household goods and load them into a freight car that would transport them from Thompson, Iowa, to Stanley, North Dakota. A few days later, the Lunds took both of their children, Amil and Millard, and climbed into a passenger car to travel in the same direction. It would be a l-o-n-g ride.

Oscar and Betsy decided to homestead west of the Missouri River between Keene and Sanish (later to be named New Town). As they headed into the unknown, they were sad about leaving their parents and many siblings behind in the Thompson area, but also excited about the new opportunities.

When they arrived on their site, they moved into a tarpaper shack built by the Iowa friends who had preceded them to North Dakota. The flat prairie — with only a few mounds of earth, called "buttes," breaking the straight line of the horizon — amazed them.

Soon, they dug an earth cellar — then, over the hole they built a four-room frame house with an enclosed back porch. This became the permanent home of the Lund's. Within three years, another son, Lester, was born. They all learned to survive through the blustery winters with severe snowstorms and the steamy summers with dust storms and swarms of various insects.

Amil learned from his father the importance of an education. Oscar was a member of the school Board for the Hawkeye Country School located one and one-half miles north of the Lund farm. Amil, also, learned through his father's example, that one must work hard to accomplish his dreams.

Betsy taught her children to be particular in the way they dressed. She expected cleanliness and orderliness. She spent hours sewing suits for her sons and husband, and crisp print dresses for herself. Even though they lived on the plains, Betsy expected everyone to be dressed in neat and prop-

Amil, Lester and Millard Lund, 1912.

er attire for each occasion. Amil dressed stylish all his life.

Amil completed his eight years of education at the one-room Hawkeye School that received its name from the township where many of the homesteaders had lived in Iowa. Amil spent the next five years assisting his father on the farm; but, all the while in his mind, he was forming plans to continue his education.

Oscar and his brother, Herman, acquired a steam engine for harvesting and named Amil "fireman." He was responsible for keeping the engine in good working order and the firebox under control.

Finally at age 20, Amil was able to fulfill his dream of furthering his education. He left for Fargo to begin high school at the North Dakota Agricultural College (NDAC), presently North Dakota State University. He completed his high school courses and graduated in 1926. Then, with determination, he continued at NDAC and graduated in 1930 with a degree in Civil Engineering.

After graduation, Amil took the train to Pennsylvania to start his job at Westinghouse's Pittsburgh plant. Within a few months the Depression had hit hard and all new employees were asked to return to their homes. Amil returned to Fargo to find a job.

Graduation photo. Amil, Millard, Lester, Oscar and Betsy Lund, 1930.

THE HOME WE SHARED

MARY AND AMIL

Amil and Mary had met before his departure to the east, and upon his return to Fargo, continued their courtship. The problem was that Amil did not have a job to support a wife. They were pleased when a job opened at the Home for someone to maintain the Home and to be a houseparent for the boys. Amil was hired, and he and Mary began making plans for their wedding.

They were married at the North Dakota Children's Home on November 12, 1930. It was the second wedding to take place in the facility. All of the children at the Home were invited. The "Fargo Forum" had this story:

A. J. LUND WEDS MARY LEAZER

North Dakota Children's Home Worker Married Here Today

Miss Mary A. Leazer, Fargo, daughter of the late Rev. and Mrs. F. E. Leazer, Sioux City, became the bride of Amil J. Lund, Fargo, at 10 a.m. today in the living room of the North Dakota Children's home, where the bride has been assistant to Superintendent H. H. Bond for several years. Rev. Earnest C. Parish, St. Paul, former pastor of the First Methodist church here, read the ring ceremony in the presence of staff members, children of the home and intimate friends.

Mrs. Bond played "The Bridal Chorus" from "Lohengrin" as the bridal party entered and also played the accompaniment for George Leazer, brother of the bride, who sang "O Promise Me." The bride wore a gown of brown silk crepe romaine, fashioned princess style with an uneven hemline. She carried a bouquet of bride's roses and baby breath. Her bridesmaid, Miss Irene M. Beck, Fargo, wore green flowered chiffon over green satin and carried tea roses and baby breath. Mrs. Bond wore a gown of ecru lace. Eloise Leazer, daughter of Mr. and Mrs. George Leazer, St. John, as flower girl dropped rose petals in the path of the bridal party. She wore a yellow organdie frock. Mr. Lund was attended by William R. Klies, Fargo, a college friend.

Following the ceremony a wedding breakfast was served in the dining room of the home. Green, gold and orchid were used in the decorations and a wedding cake centered the table. Covers were laid for 35.

Mr. Lund, the son of Mr. and Mrs. O. J. Lund of Charlson, N.D., is a graduate of the North Dakota Agricultural college. Mrs. Lund graduated from the nurses training school of Sioux City hospital, Sioux City.

Mr. and Mrs. Lund left on a trip to St. John where they will visit the brides' brother and family. They also will visit in Charlson before returning to Fargo where they will be at home at 804 Tenth St. S. after Nov. 25. Mr. Lund is supervisor of boys work in the receiving department at the Children's Home and Mrs. Lund is matron.

Mrs. Parish and Mrs. George Leazer were out of town guests.

An unexpected snowstorm that moved into the area after Veteran's Day stopped the trains, thereby shortening their honeymoon. On their return to the Home, Amil joined Mary in her one-room, with bath, apartment. They began their 24-hour a day, seven-days-a- week schedule, serving the hundreds of children that would enter and leave the facility.

Amil's engineering ability to create and organize was put to full use; he constructed cupboards, beds and mechanical items to make life more comfortable for staff and children.

The Home We Shared

Mary Leazer Lund and Amil Justine Lund's wedding photo, November, 1930.

The wedding party: Eloise Leazer Johnson was the flower girl.

The Home We Shared

Reception held in Children's Dining Room of the Home.

Mary's nursing skills were constantly needed to give the babies and children the best health care. She worked along with the community doctors, who provided free health check ups for each child.

One "night nurse" was assigned to watch over all the building and the children throughout the night. In addition, the Lunds and Miss Hartvickson, RN, who lived in a one-room apartment on the second floor, were always on 24-hour call in case of sickness or emergency.

These were the parents we shared.

Mary Leazer Lund died from a stroke on December 17, 1972 at age 75. After working 54 years for the Children's Home Society, (in later years named Children's Village and then The Village Family Service Center), Amil Justine Lund retired October 31, 1984. He died of heart failure on October 31, 1991, age 87.

The Home We Shared

Two of Amil's favorite poems and his college song (1920s):

OTHERS
by Charles D. Meigs

Lord help me live from day to day
In such a self-forgetful way,
That even when I kneel to pray,
My prayer shall be for — **others**.
Help me in all the work I do,
To ever be sincere and true,
And know that all I'd do for you
Must need be done for — **others**.
Let "Self" be crucified and slain,
And buried deep; and all in vain
May efforts be to rise again,
Unless to live for — **others**.
And when my work on earth is done,
And my new work in Heaven's begun,
May I forget the crown I've won,
While thinking still of — **others**.
Others, Lord, yes, **others,**
Let this my motto be,
Help me to live for **others,**
That I may live like Thee.

POESY UNDER 18TH AMENDMENT
(Possibly inspired by potations of home-brew) Anonymous

It was a nice day in October,
  Last September in July,
The moon lay thick upon the ground,
  The mud shown in the sky.
The flowers were singing sweetly,
  The birds were full of bloom,
So I went into the cellar,
  To sweep an upstairs room.
The time was Tuesday morning,
  On Wednesday, just at night,
I saw a thousand miles away
  A house, just out of sight.
The walls projected backwards,
  The front was round the back,
It stood alone with others,
  The fence was whitewashed black.
It was moonlight on the ocean,
  Not a streetcar was in sight,
The sun was shining brightly,
  And it rained all day that night.
It was summer in the winter,
  And the rain was falling fast.
A barefoot boy with shoes on
  Stood sitting in the grass.
It was evening and the rising sun
  Stood setting in the night.
And everything that I could see
  Was hidden from my sight.

YELLOW AND GREEN
The North Dakota Agricultural College Song
Words by A.E. Minard and Music by Dr. Putnam

1: Ho a cheer for green and yellow;
Up with yellow and the green;
They're the shades that deck our prairies,
Far and wide with glorious sheen;
Fields of waving green in springtime;
Golden yellow in the fall;
How the great high-arching heaven
Looks and laughs upon it all.

2: Here in autumn throng the nations,
Just to gather in the spoil;
Throng on freight cars from the cities;
Some to feast and some to toil;
But the yellow grain flows eastward,
And the yellow gold flows back;
Barren cities boast their plenty,
And the prairies know no lack.

3: Hushed upon the boundless prairies,
Is the bison's thundering tread.
And the Redman passes with him,
On the spoilers bounty fed;
But the Norse, the Celt, and Sason,
With their herds increase and find,
'Mid these fields of green and yellow,
Plenty e'en for all mankind.

4: Repeat verse No. 1

Note: This song is known as the college "toast." Whenever it is played by the band or sung every student rises to his feet, the men always uncovering their heads.

Amil Justine Lund

Mary Leazer Lund

25th Anniversary Photos, 1955. Photos by Dan E. Olson of Fargo.

The Home We Shared

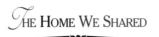

Our Shared Home

Dorothy A. Lund Nelson's Memoir of Growing Up in the North Dakota Children's Home

The Home We Shared

Fall Season (Age Birth to Five)
1933-1938

My mother, Mary, worked right through her pregnancy, quite a feat for a woman having her first child at age 36. During the summer of '33, she and my father took at least 25 children to the Holiday House on Pelican Lake. She was quite an amazing woman to have the care of all those children while being five to seven months pregnant that summer.

My birth took place on October 5, 1933, at St. John's Hospital in Fargo, North Dakota. Five days later, my father and mother brought me to their home at the North Dakota Children's Home. Our home within the Home was the original bedroom Mom had moved into in 1928; the same room that she and Dad returned to after their honeymoon. Now, they gave up a portion of the 15 by 20-foot room for a nursery.

In their large adjacent bathroom, Dad cleverly designed a hinged tabletop to fold down over the claw-foot tub forming a changing and dressing space for me. The only door from the apartment lead right out into the children's dining room.

My parents arranged their work schedule as houseparents to accommodate my daily cares. When my parents were needed in an area of the building not appropriate for a newborn or toddler, I was watched over by other staff or older youth. Raising me was a community effort and I probably spent much of my day with the children my own age as we shared parents.

Dorothy Lund, 18 months old, 1935.

As a youngster, I enjoyed the romps in the large playroom supplied with a slide, tumbling mats (old mattresses), and many toys. This room opened out onto steps that led to the well-equipped playground on the south side of the Home. Under the watchful eyes of my parents and other concerned adults, I enjoyed the fun in the outdoors, too.

Each fall, the trees on the Home's one-half block property provided a great abundance of dried leaves. The teenagers assisted my father with the raking. More than likely, he ended up raking over half of them himself.

Before "the burning of the leaves ceremony," protocol allowed the youngsters time to play in the multi-colored piles! We outlined "Houses" on the ground, with "walls" shaped to form "rooms" with "door spaces." We ran in and out of the "rooms" and "houses" with laughter and showed possessive spirits of "our domains."

The Home We Shared

Again, we formed the large piles into piles like a colorful trampoline. The other children and I jumped into and buried ourselves with great zeal. Some of the youngsters were "lost" in the leaves for a few moments.

After the leaves provided us with hours of free entertainment, it was time for Dad to gather them one last time for "the burning." At his insistence, we stood at a safe distance. Then, he ignited the colorful leaves and provided us with a fantastic bonfire! From our positions, we could feel the heat and observe the red and yellow flames consuming the leaves. The smoke sent a special odor skyward.

Around the '70s, burning of leaves was discouraged, as scientists realized pollution threatened our world. I agree with the theory, but am sad that the children of today are missing the unusual aromas that cannot be duplicated in our present society.

After all the work with the Fall leaves, Dad turned to the chore of removing all the screens from the windows both upstairs and down; replacing them with heavy storm windows. The windows were oversized, at least three and one-half by six feet. Of course, before installing the storm windows, Dad washed and polished them to the utmost.

He slid or carried them up the long ladder to the second floor. It was an event that involved the grace and balance of a tightrope walker. Then, he repeated the task using a shorter ladder for the first floor. A safe count of windows would be at least 44. I do not remember any breakage during window-changing twice yearly.

Thanksgiving

My mother adjusted my "Sunday-go-meeting" coat and bonnet. Then, she moved on to tie each of the other younger children's shoes and bonnet strings. Everyone seemed to be in a hurry. All of us were in our best outfits and it wasn't Sunday! Mrs. Layborn and Mr. Bond asked us to sit quietly on a chair by the tables in the children's dining room; yet, there were no place settings on the table, or the aroma of food from "Hansie's" kitchen.

"What at strange day!" I thought. Mom had told me to stay put on a small chair at the "little kids table," a place I did not normally sit. But I knew that if Mom said, "Sit here," I had best do so, as my parents expected obedience.

The room gradually filled with the children and teenagers. Mrs. Layborn dismissed each child through the back door. Soon, it was my turn to pass the final checkpoint. As I toddled onto the porch, I could see the children ahead of me walking down the sidewalk and climbing into a Fargo City Bus. Finally, I was assisted into the bus to join the others.

Dad announced, "We are all going out for an early Thanksgiving Dinner at the Gardner Hotel." As we exclaimed our excitement and clapped our hands, the bus started on its way. This became an annual event that continued for many years. For at least 15 years, I remember all of us children being guests of the Powers Brothers.

The Gardner Hotel was magnificent! The gigantic entrance impressed us as we approached the stairs and large glass doors. Next, we entered the large lobby with a high ceiling displaying many chandeliers! We gave many "Oohs" and "Ahs" as the splendor of lights sparkled down on us.

Then, the hotel staff greeted us and ushered us into a splendid dining room on the lower level. There, we found tables covered with white linens that flowed to the floor. Table settings of heavy silverware, long-stemmed glassware, beautiful china caught our eyes. Finally, we were seated in throne-like chairs.

"The Three Lunds," Christmas 1936.

The Gardner Hotel employees, who always seemed to give their utmost to make the children happy, served the four-course turkey dinner to us as if we were royalty. We ate until we felt a discomfort in the mid-line area of our bodies.

A special feature of this room was two opposite facing walls fully mirrored. Our images were reflected back and forth giving the sensation of looking through many rooms. We saw the groups of children repeated numerous times enjoying their meals. It displayed our great pleasure of being there.

My parents always commended the Powers Brothers for their generosity and taking such interest in the children. It was an occasion that was thoroughly enjoyed each year.

My Time Away from Home

At age four, whether it was for my personal growth or to allow my parents some time to focus completely on their work, I was taken to the Civic League Day Care twice a week. I can remember the lineup of cute

The Home We Shared

cots in the large room where we took our afternoon naps. When I was five, I went to one of the few kindergartens in the Fargo-Moorhead area. It was at Moorhead State University. The children attending were transported by taxi. Our teachers were university students doing their practice teaching.

Our Special Caretakers

Other than the hours away for day care and kindergarten, the first five years of my life were sheltered within the huge mansion. It was a lively household to grow up in. As I reflect back, I am sure that each child would have felt secure and loved by the workers.

Mr. Harold Bond, superintendent, and his wife, Brownie, lived across the alley behind the Home. He was a very loving, fatherly gentleman. His concern for each child under his care showed in his daily contacts. Brownie never complained when her husband was called in the middle of the night to assist children into their new Home.

The many other workers, house parents, cooks, laundresses, and nurses had a special relationship to each of us. They required our respect, but were tender and loving, as well.

I had the same advantage as all of the children, not only having one set of parents present each day; but also, the complete staff to be with, and my many "brothers and sisters."

During my early childhood, I learned that "life is work and work is life." I observed people serving the needs of others and not complaining about the long hours. I felt simplicity of life by living with my immediate family in a small space. I was taught that elders were to be respected and that I didn't need to be told what to do more than once. It was the generation of "children are to be seen and not heard," yet, along with that, was much love and concern. Expressing feelings was not top priority, but I did know I was cared for and loved.

A "Family Photo," 1941.

The Home We Shared

Winter Season (Age Six to 10)
1939-1943

The North Dakota Winters wrapped their chilling winds around the big mansion. Dad ordered the coal to be delivered so the bin was always filled from the middle level to the top. When the coal-man arrived, he opened the heavy steel door on a small outside window frame and placed his chute into the opening. Then, he shoveled the black nuggets onto the chute so the coal could slide down into the bin. This made a deafening sound, as the coal tumbled and hit the chute's sides.

Before winter set in, the whale of a furnace would need its annual cleaning. The furnace sat in a sunken area that looked like a waterless swimming pool. I would watch the cleaning process as my father donned some very old clothes and then disappeared into what looked like the gaping mouth of the whale. He would brush down the inside ribcage of this huge monster and bring out pails of fine dust. When Dad reappeared he was full of soot. Next, in order to clean out the pipes leading to the boiler and radiators, he ran the water out of the lines and put clean water back into them. Now, he was ready for the winter months.

The Furnace and Stoker

Fifty-degree weather meant that it was time to fill the stoker and ignite the coal in the furnace. Dad shoveled coal into the stoker, which could hold enough to feed the furnace for four to six hours. Feeding the furnace was an endless chore. Once the water in the boiler heated, it radiated the hot water throughout the Home, giving us comfortable and clean heat.

About 10 o'clock every evening, my father filled the stoker one last time and turned down the intake, which allowed the coal to move more slowly into the furnace and burn longer into the night. This sent less hot water up to the radiators so by 5 o'clock a.m., all the rooms were cool or cold. Dad was always the first person to place his feet on the cold floor, dress, and head for the basement to fill the empty belly of the stoker once again. Soon the water in the boiler was hot enough to circulate to radiators throughout the building.

Before the stoker was installed, my father had to shovel coal directly into the furnace every hour. I remember watching Dad throw the coal into the mouth of the whale. With every shovel full, it spit out flames that sprayed out and touched him. It was an extremely hot and unpleasant job, which had to be done six months of every year.

From our beds, we would start out our day listening to the clang, clang made by the temperature change in the radiators. This was a special sound of the '30s and '40s, a different musical composition each day.

By the time I was awake, my home was cozy warm. I did not appreci-

The Home We Shared

The boys built a fort.

ate enough the fact that my father's work allowed all of us to step out of bed onto a warm floor.

Dad and some of the teenage boys were blessed with the job of shoveling the snow off the half-block of sidewalks. When it snowed, they started shoveling early in the morning with never a grumble.

The boys became very creative with the snow in the yard. One year they made igloos and fort walls from hard chunks of snow. After one great snowstorm, they were even featured in "The Fargo Forum" for their creativity.

Red Stocking Project

Long before Christmas arrived, the teenagers spent their evenings assisting the office staff with the Red Stocking project. We cut little stockings with a double foot out of red construction paper. Then, we glued the foot area together in such a way as to form a small envelope. These "Red Stockings" were mailed to churches, service organizations, alumni, adoptive parents, and others across North Dakota, to remind them of the financial needs of the North Dakota Children's Home.

An accompanying letter outlined the Home's need for food, toys, clothing, baby layettes, blankets, sheets and quilts. The hope was that the Red Stockings would be returned with the envelope part containing cash gifts or checks to assist in the continuing care of the children at the Home.

The teenagers never complained about this project, as they knew the gifts would result in benefits to them. The Red Stocking project was a nice change for us from the usual study time and evening table games played after supper during the winter months. It also gave each one a sense of teamwork and accomplishment.

Filling cloth Red Stockings with fruit.

When the Red Stocking gifts began arriving, the office staff took care of the bookkeeping of all monetary donations. My mom had the responsibility of unpacking and storing all the other gifts. Dad had built clothes closets and many shelves in a large basement room. It was here that Mom hung the clothes by size and placed the toys and games on the shelves. It looked like a department store.

Each Christmas, Mrs. Laybourne and Mom made a list of all the children. Beside each name, they placed the size of clothes they presently wore and any other special needs. Then, in an exacting way, Mom matched up at least two toys and three pieces of clothing for each child. If the number of items on the shelves allowed, she selected and wrapped more gifts for the children.

The quilts that arrived were placed on the children's beds and the extra ones were stored in a second floor linen closet to be used as need-

The Home We Shared

Christmastime, 1949.

ed. The quilts were beautiful. I liked the "crazy quilts" best of all. Uneven patches of velvet, broadcloth, corduroy, and cotton were sewn on with heavy embroidery thread. The creators used many types of stitches to hold the materials together. Sometimes, the women embroidered their names onto the quilt as a message of their love to the children.

Other comforting gifts were flannel sheets that came in stripes, flowers, and pastel colors. The women's groups made them to fit the twin-size beds. We also received homemade flannel pajamas. In the coldest of nights, we could snuggle between the sheets and feel the warmth of the flannel against our bodies. The sheets and pajamas held our body heat in for the night, until we could hear the radiator's rhythmic beats in the morning.

Lion's Christmas Party

About a week before Christmas, the Lion's Club members held a festive party at the Powers Hotel. The Lions and their wives each selected one child from the Home to "adopt" for that day. The Lion couples received the special wants and needs list which Mom and Mrs. Layborn had prepared, so gifts for their selected child could be purchased ahead of the party time.

When the children arrived at the hotel, their couple met them and ushered them into a formal dining room elaborately decorated for Christmas. The couple and their child sat as a "family." The Lions were certainly upbeat men with their greetings. There was a lot of excitement and noise!

Mom, Dad, and I were invited, too. Without me seeing it happen, my parents would slip a few gifts into Santa's bag, so that I would receive

The Home We Shared

Dorothy making music, 1942.

gifts at the same time as the other children.

The hotel staff served a four-course ham or chicken Christmas dinner with all the trimmings. Dessert was a square of ice cream with a colored design within the white trim, a red Santa, blue bell, or green Christmas tree. We wondered how the dairy could make these fancy treats.

After the meal, the program began with introductions, Christmas carols, and the mighty roars from the Lions. Each year, I was asked to play a few songs on my accordion.

Next, a few verses of "Jingle Bells" brought Santa Claus with his huge packs and boxes. Santa called out names of the youngsters and distributed the gifts from the Lion couples. Then, the Christmas paper began to fly about the room. The children were pleased with the gifts they received and thanked their host family. The Lions and their wives showed great compassion and appeared to be having as great a time as the children. I remember this as a most joyful and marvelous occasion.

Christmas at Home

During the Christmas season, the first floor rooms of the Home were beautifully decorated. An eight-foot fur tree brightened a corner of the Children's Dining Room and my father placed a wooden "fireplace" he had built in the front hallway. Christmas scenes and lights adorned every hutch and extra shelf. The children knew Christmas was right around the corner. Many, also, took part in choir concerts and programs at their churches and schools.

On Christmas Eve, Fiesta dishes were lowered from their high cupboards to be set on the children's tables. The hues of pink, yellow, aqua, green, and blue brightened the tables where 50 or more would eat.

Hansie, the cook, prepared a delicious meal. Actually, all of her meals were delicious. After enjoying a turkey dinner, the girls assigned to cleanup would hurry to clear the tables and wash the dishes. On Christmas Eve the crew worked fast, as they were anxious for the party to start.

Finally, the bell rang and we all gathered around the tree. After we heard the Christmas Story and sang carols, Santa arrived. His pack was always filled to the top, and large boxes of gifts were slid into the room from the front hall "sleigh." The children were excited by all the wonderful surprises they received when Santa called their names. All of the gifts came from contributors across North Dakota, Minot to Wahpeton, Mott

THE HOME WE SHARED

to Grand Forks!

I believe the Home was able to meet the needs of the children for clothes and toys — thanks to its generous contributors. In most cases, the children received as much for Christmas as their classmates who came from average income homes. However, their greatest desire — a visit from their parents — often remained unmet. Although the caring staff and peer friendships couldn't take the place of their parents, they could assist them through the pain of the unfulfilled wish. The children felt love and concern that continued throughout the year.

Many other organizations gave of their time and large gifts of money to the Society. Some of them were the Rotary Club, Masonic Lodge, Eastern Star, and Shriners.

Christmas, 1949.

Christmas, 1946.

THE HOME WE SHARED

World War II

One dark part of these winter years was World War II. Because my dad was too old to be drafted, he elected in 1942 to serve his country by moving to Portland, Oregon, to work in the shipyards. Those days without my father and hearing all the war news on radio were filled with fear. Often, we had to participate in "Air Raids" at school and "Black Outs" at home. The Home staff, under Mom's guidance, had an immense task to cover each of the 44 or more windows with blackening materials. Then, we had to shut off all the lights and remain quiet. The blackout supervisors, men assigned to various areas of Fargo, took their places in our neighborhood during the air raids and told us whether or not we had passed the inspection.

A few months later, Dad returned to Fargo, as he could not tolerate the cold, damp weather in Seattle. I think he was lonesome, too. How happy I was to have him back home. Yet his absence was a good lesson for me, helping me to understand the losses the children were going through.

The war brought a new diet to the Home in the form of Army Surplus commodities. Three-foot high barrels of dried eggs and powdered milk arrived, along with canned meat, vegetables, and fruit. Hansie continued to create great meals and none of us went hungry. Most likely, we were the first kids in town to consume scrambled eggs from the powdered form.

The Lund's Kitchen

We ate most of our meals in the staff dining room with the other workers. However, two to four times a month, we had a meal alone as a family, in our kitchen. Dad had built this kitchen in the southwest corner of the basement, just off of his tool and workroom.

Dad placed a cupboard and counter with a set-in sink on one wall,

The Lund's kitchen, 1939.

The Home We Shared

Dorothy baked a cake for her Mom's birthday.

Amil ready for a meal prepared by Mary.

above them he hung more cupboards. A small gas stove set beside the cupboards. A small table and four chairs were placed in the center of this room. One window to the south added a bit of light.

Here my family could have a meal with selected guests. When the visitors or relatives arrived, they were guided from our apartment, through the children's dining room, down the stairs to the basement, past the older boys work/play area, around the furnace, through Dad's tool room, and finally into our kitchen-dining area. Our guests had a long way to "go out for dinner" from our apartment.

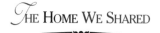

Photo Laboratory

This kitchen area doubled as a photo developing dark room. Dad assisted relatives by taking their photos and printing them on "Christmas Cards" for their Christmas letters. Mom became his assistant in the development process, and both held membership in the Fargo Camera Club.

Even more important for Dad was taking photos of the children. His goal was to take a photo of every child that entered the Home, but he realized during his first year working at the Home that he couldn't possibly achieve his goal. He took photos as he had time and left a picture legacy of the Home and its children.

The Winter Season years taught me the meaning of the word "fear." I often worried about arriving home safely from school, scared that an air raid or attack would occur while I was in route. At that time, I didn't quite understand how far away the war action was taking place. I had the comfort and shelter of my Home, and the friendships with my peers, though I realized they would come and go as they were adopted or placed in foster care. Now, I began to wonder if I, too, had been adopted; though I had the features and coloring of my dad, I certainly did not look like my mother! As an adult, I now realize I have her personality.

The Home We Shared

Spring Season (Ages 11 to 15)
1944-1948

Spring brought much activity within the Home. It was a time to prepare for Easter. Each child attended the church of its birth family preference. When a child was considered for adoption, even the adoptive parents were selected not only to match the educational and cultural background of the birth parents, but, also, the religious preference. There were many churches in Fargo involved in the children's religious growth. These churches provided transportation for the children to and from church events.

Easter

The Easter I remember best, was in 1945 when it fell on April 1st, April Fool's Day. Mom, who had a great sense of humor, gathered some of us older girls around her and taught us how to blow out the inside of an egg without breaking the shell. We punched a small hole in each end of the shell and blew hard to push the yolk and white out of the egg. Then she made a soft soap solution we poured back into the eggs. In a short time it had set, so that later when someone cracked the egg it would appear to be hard-boiled! Next, we covered small pieces of cardboard and sponge with chocolate, so they looked like pieces of candy. What fun we had giving these out on Easter afternoon to the older boys!

One Easter, we had a severe blizzard that lasted three days! We could not even see the houses and store across 10th Street. When it finally stopped snowing, it took Dad and the teenage boys many days to shovel out the long sidewalk. I was selected along with one of the boys to

Snowbanks after the April 1st blizzard, 1945.

Myra and Dorothy after a snowstorm.

walk over snowdrifts pulling a sled with a box on it. Our destination was a small grocery store near Agassiz school — about four blocks away on 13th Street. Our mission was to buy milk, eggs and bread for the Home. It was an extremely cold mission to accomplish.

Another Easter I remember well, was the one on which I received my last spanking! Our family had returned from church and I was asked to practice the piano. I thought, "I should have a complete vacation," and told my mother that fact. Well, a few swats on the rear impressed me enough to settle in at the piano.

I was embarrassed when it was time for our family to walk to the staff dining room because I knew the children gathered in the dining room for Easter Dinner had heard the commotion through our apartment door. They all knew I had been spanked! I made a sheepish walk through their dining area.

The Home We Shared

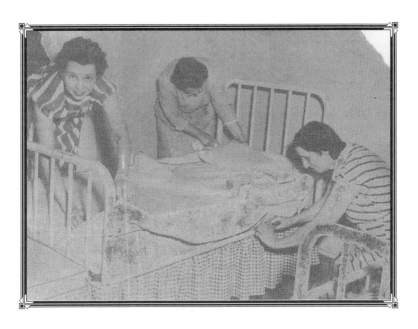

These picture come from an article in "The Fargo Forum," 1950s.

WOMEN DECORATING YOUNG GIRLS' DORMITORY

Top: Quilted peach-colored spreads, corded in apricot, with "shirts" in apricot, peach and white, deck each little bed and the chest at the foot. Pictured left to right are Dorothy Ztechka, Ruth Dawson, and Ruth Ranstad.

Right: Frilly curtains are hung by Miss Wright and Miss Tveiten.

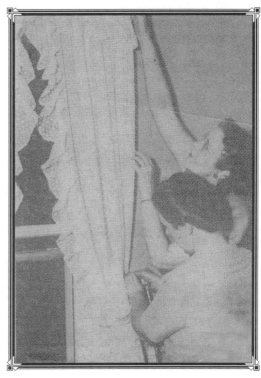

St. Patrick's Day

Mom always celebrated St. Patrick's Day. She thought that some of her ancestors had come from Ireland. She knitted an olive-green two piece dress for me to wear, each spring, on the big day! It didn't matter that I had grown two to three inches over a year, as she would simply knit the number of inches needed onto the waist of the blouse and hem of the skirt. Thus, for many years this outfit and I were designated to show her heritage to the community.

Whenever Mom found a few minutes to sit down in our apartment, she picked up her knitting needles or crochet hook and created baby sweaters, booties, caps and blankets. It was amazing how quickly a layette was completed. Many babies wore these outfits as they left the Home with their new parents.

Spring, also, brought the complete window-changing event, again! Now, Dad would work at sliding the heavy storm windows down the two-story wooden ladder, and replace them with screens. Often, he had to repair screens that had weakened or been damaged by little fingers.

A Child with Special Needs

In the spring of 1945, an 11-month-old Native American, Marlene, was brought to the Home. She appeared to be quite ill and many parts of her body had open sores. She was placed in the Toddler Nursery and my mother began to watch over her physical condition.

Mom covered Marlene's hands with puffy mittens to keep her from scratching her itching body. With the help of many doctors and tests, they discovered she had eczema, and was allergic to most clothing and foods.

Our two-room apartment within the Home.

Mom turned to a rice or barley cereal diet and linen clothes for the child, along with using the internal medicines, ointments and dressings prescribed by the doctor. Sometimes, she appeared to be wrapped like a mummy. By feeding her the few items she could tolerate and slowly adding other foods or clothing items, eventually she was healed. This was the type of treatment all children with special needs received at the Home. Mom took many of these children "under her wing," even after retiring from the staff at the Home.

Now I have a sister!

Myra and buster, 1946.

My Sister

Mom and Dad developed a close attachment to Marlene as Mom's constant care of this child continued over two years. Marlene spent many hours in our apartment and joined the children at the lake the summer she was two. Finally, my parents asked to adopt her. After they completed the paper work and paid the $35 fee, the adoption was complete. She was named, "Myra Dean Lund." I now had a REAL sister!

Because this was one of the first cross-racial adoptions, none of us knew how difficult it would be for Myra to be raised in Fargo, a predominately white community. Myra was one of the few Native American children to attend public school in Fargo. I remember feeling angry when people would say, "Look at that cute Indian girl!" She was MY SISTER!

Since there were now four of us living in the one room apartment, Mr. Bond directed that an additional room be built on to the back of the Home. Now, Myra and I had our own bedroom! Our double rollaway bed was folded up against a wall in the daytime to allow more space for play and study. We both had large doll collections. Dad built in cupboards, closets, bookshelves and desk on one wall. We enjoyed this special room, just for us. Even though we were 10 years apart in our ages, we went everywhere together. We were the best of pals.

Attending School

The children from the Home attended Hawthorne Elementary School located at 4th Street and 9th Avenue South, about six blocks east of the Home. Presently, the old school houses the "Evaluation Training Center." The children were well accepted and made up about a fourth of each class. Since they attended school in a large group, they could defend each other if ever there was a need.

After grade school, we attended Agassiz Junior High School, a three-block walk to the west. Agassiz Junior High offered well-trained teachers in each area of study. Students passed from room to room to have the best-qualified teacher in that course. We participated in physical education exhibitions showing our abilities in gymnastics, dancing, team

Six teenagers on their way to junior or high school, 1950s.

The Home We Shared

games, and marching. When high school age, all went to Fargo Central high School about seven blocks to the north on 10th Street.

So the children would do well in school, the Home staff guided the youth in their studies each evening. The children gathered in the dining room and library to prepare their homework. The library had a great selection of books and encyclopedias to use for preparing reports for school projects. When we finished our homework, the table games would begin. Parcheesi and Monopoly were two of our favorites. We played card games such as "Go to the Dump" and "Old Maid."

Since all girls took Home Economics in Junior High, I began to take an interest in sewing and cooking. My mother was an excellent seamstress, so the two of us spent many hours creating my new outfits or mending clothes for the Home.

The Lund family, 1948.

When I found an interesting recipe that could be made on a hot plate, the fold down table over our tub became the "kitchen" counter. It was the very same table used as a dressing table for Myra and I as toddlers.

During my Junior High years, I slowly moved away from the close relationships at the Home and began to form new relationships through school and church.

A Potluck group was one activity I enjoyed. For me, it began at Agassiz Junior High School and continued through graduation from Fargo Central High School. Eight girls from the same orchestra class at school would gather on Friday evenings at one of the girl's homes. The hosting family furnished the casserole or "hot dish." The rest of us brought an assigned item, such as, salad, milk, bread, trimmings or dessert. When it was my turn to hostess the group, we worked around the meals served at the Home and had our potluck meal in the Staff Dining Room.

Church Activities

The Methodist Youth Fellowship at First United Methodist Church offered me opportunities to grow in faith, leadership and fellowship. The group became very important to me. Here is where I realized my leadership skills — skills that had formed through my experiences of living at the Home.

The Youth Fellowship held some social activities at the Home. I was often asked to hostess the group of 20 or more, as I had the largest home of all the members! I think my parents appreciated the new friendships I was forming. They realized these friendships would be longer lasting than the temporary ones formed at the Home.

Illnesses

When I was 11, my mother became ill and was hospitalized. I was told she had the "flu." Each day, my father delivered my creative "get well cards" to her. Then, one day at school the principal, Mr. Brown, asked me if my mother needed more blood, as he had the same type. I was in shock, as I had not been told the seriousness of her illness. Many weeks later, she returned to our Home and was soon back to work.

A few months later, my dad took his turn in the hospital. Thus, Mr. Bond had to take over my father's jobs within the Home. These are the only times that I recall my parents being ill.

The Lund family, 1951.

Employment

My very first "job" was to go door-to-door selling a small can (like a shoe polish can) of salve. The salve was a cure for everything. Skin rash, burns, itch, etc. I'm sure it was once sold by the traveling medicine men! I did not do well at these sales, but I know that we used many cans of this salve in our own family.

At some point, I became an employee of the Home and earned small amounts of money — possibly it came from my parents. I helped fold clothes in the laundry. Sometimes, I ironed and distributed the clothes to the proper closets.

As I got older, I assisted in the nurseries, sterilizing baby bottles, preparing formula, filling the bottles, and feeding the babies.

In addition to working at the Home, I had the privilege to be promoted from taking dance and baton lessons at the Shippey School of Dance to being one of her instructors. Thus, after school two to three times a week, I would teach tap and ballet to the younger children. Then, every Saturday morning I taught baton twirling to all of her students. This was a good way for me to earn a little

Mrs. Shippey and Dorothy at Mrs. Shippey's School of Dance, 1951.

money. It was very inconvenient, however, when I wanted to participate in "sleepovers" which the potluck group would have quite often. I was the only one who had to arise early on Saturday morning and be at work.

Springtime was a growing time for me. I was well involved in the Home activities — still leading the playroom activities, studying with others in the library, playing softball, anti-I-over, and wrestling with the teenagers. At the same time, I was drawing away from Home children and staff as I made new friends outside the Home.

Myra and I were developing our sisterhood and enjoying it. As I look back, I feel that it was more like a mother-daughter relationship. Regardless of the name to be given to the relationship, it made both of us happy.

At church, I spent time planning worship services, acting in skits, and going to camp with the MYF youth. Our youth director, Augie Aamout, was a most outstanding leader and guided us in our activities.

When I wanted "time away" I simply went to the Home's Library, selected a book or magazine, and curled up on a window seat to read. One of my favorite books was "Daddy Long Legs" by Jean Webster, written in 1912. I still enjoy reading it.

The Home We Shared

Mother and Myra.

Mom and Dad continued to divide their time between all their responsibilities to the children of the Home and raising their two daughters. Our parents saw that we had dance, baton, and piano lessons. Myra even became a figure skater. It was an extremely busy life for our parents.

Myra died July 11, 1984 at age 40 of Liver Disease.

The Home We Shared

Summer Season (Ages 16 to 22)
1949-1955

The sun awoke me as it stretched its warm beams around the cottage at Camp Watson. I had a great view of each day's dawn, because my bed was located in the northwest corner of the front porch with windows at the head and one side. Glass windows started three feet off the porch floor and could be slid open to allow the flow of fresh air.

The L-shaped porch was the sleeping area for the teenage girls. All of us could see nature from our beds — the morning sun breaking over the back of the cottage, the dark clouds rolling in from the west with a storm, the branches of the trees swaying in the wind, and the colors of many wonderful sunsets.

Often, our sleep was disturbed by high winds slapping the rain against the windows, bright streaks of lightning brightening the porch area, or thunder rumbling so loud it shook the window frames. These storms came up quickly across Pelican Lake. On those nights, I was afraid and crawled down into my bed with the blankets over my head! Though we never talked about it, I'm sure the other girls did the same.

To be at Camp Watson for the three months of summer was a wonderful experience. The 25 to 30 children who lived at the North Dakota Children's Home were brought from Fargo to be immersed with the true magnitude of nature.

Though it was a summer camping experience, my parents, the only adults present, brought order to the days. They had the total responsibility for all of the children — their health care, food, swimming lessons, clean clothes and daily schedule.

Quiet Time for Our Mom and Dad

Mom and Dad would arise at least an hour before they awoke the children. They took their daily "morning dip" in the lake and they spent time together reading their devotional books and setting out the plan for the day.

Because the older boys filled the wood box each evening, Dad could fill the cook-stove and ignite the wood. He then used a pitcher to carry water from the pump to the stove. It took him many trips across the kitchen to fill the reservoir. After breakfast, the water was hot enough to wash the dishes.

At the same time, Mom would begin the breakfast. She would stir up muffin or coffee cake recipes and pour them into the large cake pans to be baked. Many types of hot cereal were also on the menu, Oatmeal, Ralstons, Cream of Wheat and even Corn Meal Mush.

These few minutes were one of the two times each day that my parents had together without children around them. The other would be after all the children were tucked into bed for the night.

The Home We Shared

The Morning Schedule

The childrens' day began to the ring of a school bell, the signal that it was time to wake up and arise for a new day of activity. As a teenager, it was my job to assist in bed making, especially taking care of the sofa beds. The other teenage girls and I folded blankets and sheets, placing them into the wood framed storage area under the davenports. Then, we latched them in a forceful manner, making the night's bed into a sitting place for the daytime.

The teenagers led the younger children to their respective "bath houses." The girls' bathhouse, which had been built by Dad, looked like a large garage. Benches extended along two walls, and above the benches were hooks for clothes. In the winter, this bathhouse doubled for a boathouse. The large rowboat and pieces of the dock were housed here to keep them from the snow and ice. The boys' bathhouse was much older and smaller. It had been on the grounds when the camp was donated to the Home.

Girls at Camp Watson. Mary Lund is in the back row, second from the left, 1950.

In the bathhouse, we all put on our swimsuits and came out racing towards the beach area. It was our turn for the brisk "morning dip!" We would jump quickly into the water to rinse off our bodies, race back to the bathhouse, dry ourselves, get dressed, and hang the bathing suits on lines outside each bathhouse.

During the '30s and '40s, the "morning dip" was a popular health procedure. The dip was noted in health books as "good for the body," so we were expected to participate. It was a way to have everyone bathe himself or herself, as there was no other source of water except for the one kitchen pump, which provided drinking water.

Some of the children were on a "bladder training program," meaning Mom woke them at night to use the china chamber pots in the various bedrooms. Even with these precautions some would wet their bed. When this occurred, the bedding was carried to the lake to be washed. This became another task for us teenagers. We would slush the bedding in the lake water. Then, go on shore. Two of us stood facing each other and twisted the material in opposite directions, ringing the water out of the bedding. Finally, we went off to the back yard to hang them on the clotheslines behind the cottage.

Enjoying the Outdoors

The summer dress code was simple! I'm sure it made the Monday washday more tolerable for my parents. Also, they believed that a suntan was healthy! The unisex apparel was only a pair of shorts. Later, as the girls matured a halter-top was added. On cool days, we wore slacks and shirts. For gentle rainy days with no lightning, we donned our swimsuits, so we could run in the rain, splatting our feet in the large puddles!

If weather permitted, we ate in the great outdoors. Breakfast, lunch, and supper became a "picnic" at two long wooden tables. Dad and assigned teenagers carried the food 60 feet from the cottage kitchen to a serving table. Mom dished the food onto the individual plates and one of the children placed the plates on the table. It was amazing that there was just enough for everyone. Mom seemed to know how much to place on each plate. Many times, she offered seconds to the older youth.

Playing house, 1943.

Cod Liver Oil and Tooth-Brushing Time

After eating our hot cereal, hot bread, fruit, and milk, it was time to line up for our teaspoon of cod liver oil. Each of us had to bring our cup or glass with water to wash it down. Then, we walked to the toothbrush stand and retrieved our toothbrush. The stand had a row of cup hooks on one layer, a small shelf, and then another row of cup hooks below the shelf. Each hook was numbered. A variety of colored toothbrushes hung on the hooks.

It was important to remember your number and color of toothbrush. Dad poured water from a pitcher into glasses and then Mom placed in our hand a small amount of "homemade toothpowder," a mixture of salt and baking soda. If this balancing act was too difficult, we could place the glass on the small shelf. We simply dipped our toothbrushes into the water, then the toothpowder, and finally into our mouths for brushing.

Of course, as we grew older, we found that instead of spitting on the ground, we could accidentally spit on someone's bare foot or at a selected target with the winner receiving a cheer.

Chores To Do

The teenage girls cleaned off the tables and took the dishes into the kitchen to be washed. We took the hot water from the stove reservoir and placed it into two large aluminum dishpans. In one, we sloshed around a small metal soap holder to make bubbles and the washing began.

The older boys had their chores, too. These included cutting firewood, stacking it in neat piles near the barn and shed, carrying some to the kitchen wood box, and sweeping the sand that had been brought in on the boy's bare feet up the stairway and across the floors of the upstairs bedrooms.

Playtime

If it wasn't your turn to be working in the cottage, you were assigned to watch the younger children and assist with setting up the play areas. We spread old blankets on the ground and placed dollhouse furniture on them. We put pails, cars, dump trucks, sand conveyors, and shovels on the beach. For the older children, we brought out the bats, balls, stilts, and tools.

The children played with great imagination. The blanket areas became "houses" with all the children taking turns "playing house." Lilac leaves and sand mixed with a small amount of water became peanut butter sandwiches for the dolls, stones became various fruits and vegetables, and pieces of wood were spoons and forks. We would catch minnows and serve up a fish dinner to the dolls.

When we discovered walking sticks, tadpoles, frogs, toads, lizards, butterflies, moths and the variety of minnows, we could touch, look, and observe the uniqueness of each specimen.

Even the dead, decaying state of nature was studied, as we checked out what had washed ashore after a storm. We found many types of fish, dogfish, and loons. It was most impressive to see up close the loon's checkerboard looking feather layers of black and white! After studying the dead animals washed up on shore, it was time for the burial. Finding the right place for the burial was usually Dad's job. We children stood in reverence for the occasion.

Swimming Lessons

Swimming consumed most of each day. In addition to the "morning dip," there was an hour of swimming each morning, afternoon, and evening. Mom and Dad were the swimming instructors and lifeguards for the group. It was amazing that they set up an excellent water safety system without any Water Safety Instruction courses. My parents created separate roped off areas for three levels of swimmers, and tested the children on their abilities before allowing them into a deeper area.

They would not allow anyone to go to the raft or diving tower without first swimming many yards parallel to the shoreline. Once you proved your strength and ability in strokes, you were allowed to swim to the raft and dive out over the drop-off. This was the ultimate dream for each child regardless of age. Even some five year olds reached this goal.

During these summer months, all of the children learned to be very strong swimmers and could swim long distances. In all the years at the lake, even with so many children present, there was only one near drowning. One small child had gone into the water in a "non-swimming area." Fortunately, one of our neighbors was boating by and saw the child. He yelled with great excitement, pointing towards the boat dock

Learning to swim at Camp Watson.

Mary giving diving lessons.

area, and continued to call out to my parents.

Mom ran to the area and soon was carrying a small dripping wet child up the boat landing. She assisted the child with breathing, which caused the child to spit and cough. The near drowning would not have occurred had the child kept the rules of the camp to "stay out of the water until swim time and only then go in at the beach area." My parent's discipline, expectations, and system kept an astonishing "no drowning safety record" over the many years!

My parents knew how to dog paddle, sidestroke, backstroke and dive. Thus, when I entered Fargo Central High School swim classes, I was the speediest dog paddling person in the class. I had been doing that stroke for the previous 12 years during all the summer's months. Because of this love for the water and swimming, I concentrated on the water skills, various strokes, and Life Saving techniques in high school. I was able to pass the Water Safety Instructor's course by age 17. I gave up my summers at Camp Watson and became a Lifeguard and Swimming Instructor at the Island Park Swimming Pool for a number of summers. That gave me the opportunity to earn money for college.

Afternoon at Camp Watson

Lunch at Camp Watson consisted of sandwiches, drinks, and fruit. The sandwiches came in a variety of flavors — plain peanut butter, peanut butter and jelly, peanut butter with cut up onions (it tastes like nuts), egg salad, and tuna salad,

After the lunch cleanup and tooth brushing time, EVERYONE took a nap, usually on a blanket spread out on the grass. Resting spots were in the shade of the great trees all around the yard. The trees provided automatic air conditioning for the afternoon siesta.

It is interesting that the National Camping Association presently requires camp schedules to have a FOB — "Feet On Bed" time scheduled.

The Home We Shared

The boys with tools at Camp Watson, 1950.

This association realizes that children need a quiet time to maintain their health throughout the week or month of camping. This "siesta" was observed during the three months at Camp Watson by the leadership of my parents without any regulations from a state or national association.

After the "siesta," came afternoon snacks with a fruit drink, graham crackers or cookies. Then, the afternoon hours allowed for more playtime, and another hour of swimming. Later, it was time for the "picnic" supper that would consist of goulash or a meat product, vegetables, bread, fruit, and desert. Mom prepared all cooked items in eight-quart kettles or large rectangular pans on or in the wood stove. Usually, there were "seconds" for everyone who wished to have more food. Then again, came the cleanup and tooth-brushing time.

Evening Activities

In the evenings, there were group games, such as kickball, tag, red rover, and streets and alleys. Stilt walking contests began as three or four youth tried to walk from the barn all around the cottage and back to the barn before falling off their stilts as all of us cheered for them.

Dad joined them and was one of the best! At age 70 in 1973, he even demonstrated his skill for his grandsons. At that time, he could swing himself up onto the stilts from the ground. His grandsons had to use the

The Home We Shared

Reading hour in the cottage, 1943.

back porch to step off onto the stilt as their starting point.

Very hot evenings warranted another "dip" in the lake! Sometimes "skinny dipping" was allowed in non-mixed groups.

When darkness covered the camp, we moved indoors for a variety of activities. The choices were playing table games in the dining area, listening and dancing to the Edison Phonograph records on the front porch, reading the Big-Little Books that were stored behind the living room doors, or listening to the radio. After electricity arrived at the lake, our lone radio was perched in a window space between the kitchen and the dining room. This was our only source of world news.

On cold days and nights, Dad built a fire in the living room fireplace and we sat around it to enjoy the heat. Sometimes the long handled popcorn maker was taken down from the wall so we could pop corn and share the treat. Occasionally, we roasted marshmallows. Sometimes, I would take out my accordion and we'd have a sing-along.

Bedtime

All too soon, it would be bedtime for the young children. They were escorted by flashlight to the outhouses. There were two outhouses, one for the boys, another for the girls. These were located on the back corners of the yard, at least 70 feet from the house. Definitely, this night walk was not one that young children would want to take by themselves. I thought the boys had the darkest path to travel, as it was under a thick stand of trees.

The outhouses hold many funny stories. One that was a most difficult time for Dad, was when a young boy on his evening jaunt set the flashlight down on the board seat in the area between the two holes. While he was using one hole, the flashlight rolled into the unused hole! A flashlight and batteries were "worth their weight in gold," and had to be retrieved! Somehow, Dad made a lasso and hook retriever so that the glowing item could be brought back up out of the hole. After being cleaned thoroughly, it was used many more times.

Later in the evening, the older youth took their walk to the outhouses and then settled into bed. The girls would have to open up the davenports, pull the bedding from the box underneath, and unfold the daven-

The Home We Shared

Marshmallows around the fireplace.

port to make a double bed, and place the sheets and blankets on top. Now they had a place to sleep. The older boys simply went to their cots in the upstairs bedrooms.

Boating

Sometimes we took a LONG boat ride around Pelican Lake. So that there would be a place for each child to sit, our large motor (row) boat would tow a second smaller rowboat. Slowly, we would skirt the edge of the lake, go through the straits, and follow the shoreline of the larger part of Pelican Lake. This was definitely an all day trip, so we took lunch and fishing gear along. As we moved slowly, a few fish would be caught, but most of the time was spent viewing the various styles of cottages, speedboats, and rafts. We enjoyed waving and yelling "hellos" in response to the greetings from the many onlookers on the shore.

Dad had only one boating accident in all those years! He had taken some of the boys fishing by way of the swampy river that connected our lake to Little Pelican Lake. As the boat was moving through the marshes of the river channel, one of the boys saw a turtle on a log. He jumped up to point it out to the others and said, "Look at the Turtle!"

Well, "boys will be boys" and all wanted to see it, so they too jumped up and moved to the edge of the boat for a better look at the turtle. Unfortunately, the boat tipped to that side, tossing Dad and his crew into the water! Thank goodness, it was a shallow area and the swimming classes had paid off, as everyone returned to the boat safely. After climbing back in, they had to use old coffee cans to bail out the water. The rule

A sunset on Lake Pelican as seen from Camp Watson.
Devils Slide is the hill at the far right.

of "do not stand up in a boat" had to be reviewed and obeyed on the future boat trips!

The teenagers enjoyed frequent trips to Devil's Slide, a very high cliff on the north side of our section of the lake. It had a steep sandy drop off towards the water. It was fun to climb to the top of the cliff and walk back onto the grassy knoll about 20 feet away from the drop off. Then, we'd take a running start; jump off the cliff, and land on the soft sandy slope with repeated jumps, slides, and leaps to the bottom. Of course, this stimulating downward adventure encouraged us to repeat the climb to the top, the running start, and leaps down the sandy slide, again and again!

We also traveled by land. The road that circled to the south edge of the lake was at least five miles long. This was a half-day's journey to hike, look over the area and have a snack. Sometimes we followed the shoreline, but this was an uncomfortable way to travel. The stones were most difficult to walk on with our bare feet for the long distance.

Traveling on the road towards the north, one could easily hike for ten miles. This brought a view of resorts, one-room schoolhouse, farms and a Catholic Church. Hiking consumed hours of our time.

24 Hours a Day, 7 Days a Week

The summer activities, as seen through the eyes of children, were fun and easy. It was a most free style of living! For Mom and Dad, the summer activities had to be WORK! During the three months, they were responsible for the large family of children and youth, 24 hours a day, seven days a week. The most difficult jobs must have been washday, food preparation, and wood chopping.

The Home We Shared

Unless it was raining, every Monday was washday. Early in the morning, Dad filled the reservoir on the stove plus two large copper wash kettles with cold water. When the wood fire had heated the water to a hot level, it was transferred by bucket to the all-purpose room just off the kitchen. There the water was dumped into the washing machine with a small gas motor. In later years, an electric motorized wringer-type machine replaced it.

All of the towels, sheets, and clothes were washed in the small machine; rung through a hand turned ringer, which later was motorized, too. Then, Mom and Dad carried clothesbaskets full of wet laundry out to the "Monday clothes lines," which had been strung up around all the available trees on the north side of the yard. Clothes and bedding for this group of people made quite a colorful sight throughout the yard!

There was a complete division of labor, between Mom and Dad. Dad carried the hot water to the machines and together, they washed the clothes. Then, he carried the heavy clothesbaskets to the lines, and Mom hung the clothes on the lines. At the end of the day, they removed the clothes from the lines, folded them, made beds, and put the clothes away. The teenagers assisted with these tasks. Finally, Dad removed the clotheslines, leaving only a short line for wet swimsuits or dishtowels used during the week.

Supplies

Many items of food, especially the staples, were brought to Camp Watson at the beginning of the summer. These were stored on the built in shelves in the multi-purpose room that also housed the washing machine, rinse tubs, and icebox. Dad bought groceries for our weekly needs in Detroit Lakes. He used the Camp Watson Model A Ford for all the shopping, so had replaced the rumble seat with a large wooden box trunk. This made the Ford into a small pickup truck. Once a week he drove into town to buy fresh produce, meat and medical supplies.

As the staples ran out, Lucy Hall, a social worker from the Home, brought new supplies from Fargo to the lake. Sometimes, she would bring a new child out for the remaining summer days and/or return to Fargo with a child that was to be adopted. Lucy's arrival always brought some special treats — root beer barrels, candy corn, or gumdrops! But, most of all, we knew her arrival meant a change in at least one child's life.

Dad also used the Model A to retrieve ice for the icebox. It was exciting to go to a nearby farm and watch the men push the sawdust off a layer of ice and extract a huge square of ice from that level. If it was too large for our box, they would saw the hunk into smaller pieces.

It amazed me to realize that all this ice could stay in that barn during the hot summer and be available for us to keep our food cold through the three months. When we first went for ice in early summer, the men would be taking ice from near the ceiling of the barn. As we returned

The Home We Shared

Lucy Hall's visit — Mary Lund serving food.

each week, the levels of ice became much lower to the ground. Somehow, there was always enough for the season.

Preparing Meals

There must have been only a few hours a day that food preparation was not happening in the cottage! Meals were well balanced from the five food groups. It is difficult for me to understand how my parents knew what time to start the wood stove fire in order to have items baked on time for a meal. Especially when they were working with such large amounts of food.

Dad's specialty was making pancakes. Once a week he took over that job. He placed the batter in a metal pitcher and poured the exact amount onto the grill so they were of uniform size and shape.

Maintaining the yard and buildings was another endless task. The yard was mowed with a push mower. The cottage of white with blue trim was a gem, but required continual paint and repair.

Dad built a walk-in, small house with built-in sink, stove, and cupboards for the young children. He fashioned cute tables, chairs, and benches. The children often carried pieces of furniture out to the "blanket houses," and developed a village. Later, he built a small barn and windmill near by. These added "on the farm" imaginary times.

Medical Needs

Because of Mom's nursing training, she was aware of the children's medical needs. She treated the usual scrapes, cuts, poison ivy, colds, and sunburns. When a child became extremely ill, Dad drove to a nearby resort and phoned Doctor Lancaster at his cottage across Pelican Lake. The doctor arrived in his speedboat. Other times, Dr. Lancaster glided smoothly to our dock in his sailboat. Those times he would check on the condition of all the children. After the checkups, he would offer rides in either of his boats. The children enjoyed the visits from this wonderful doctor.

"Amil's Farm" at Camp Watson, 1939.

Polio

One summer a polio epidemic swept through the midwest and all of the home workers were concerned for the health of the children. To everyone's amazement, none of the special children at the Home contracted polio.

We children at Camp Watson remained polio-free, as well. In fact, due to the epidemic, we were given an "extended vacation" that year, so that we would not be near children who had contracted polio. The Fargo schools opened later that fall and we remained at Camp Watson, enjoying our usual schedule.

My summers spent at the lake were the most meaningful time of each year. It was a time of natural freedom in one of the most beautiful places. I grew to appreciate sharing the workload along with the fun. As a teenager, I was only treated differently from the rest of the children, in

The Home We Shared

"The Potluck" on graduation day from Fargo Central High School, 1951. Back row: Margaret Forthun, Carol Bailey, Sandra Puckering, and Sally Maynard. Middle row: Dorothy Lund, Virginia Pratt, Gretchen Muehlenbein, and Margaret Otterson. Front row: Jane Heifort and Barbara Sorlien.

the fact that I could stay up a little later and be alone with my parents for a short time in the evening. I used these quiet times to sew on an old treadle machine, preparing my wardrobe for the next school year. Otherwise I was expected, just like the other teenagers, to take my turn at washing the dishes and taking care of the younger children.

These responsibilities were placed on me during my Junior and Senior High years, and were skills I would use often in the future. I think the years at the lake influenced me most in my choice of vocation. After graduating from Fargo Central High School, I lived in Fargo in order to teach swimming and be a lifeguard at the Island Park Swimming Pool.

Physical education and recreation seemed a natural, too! My whole life had been directing activities, such as: games, playtime, and swimming. Now, I had decided to learn the why of it all. Why was leisure time and re-creation instead of wreak-creation important?

As I began to attend North Dakota Agricultural College (presently, North Dakota State University) in Fargo, I no longer had the many contacts with the children, neither at the Home nor at Camp Watson.

Beginning in the fall of 1951 and until I finished college in 1955, our family of four lived in the two-story house behind the Home. It was the first time we had a place of our own. This house was formerly used for a

The Home We Shared

staff residence or to isolate children who were sick.

Mom took on new responsibilities, as she became a transporter of babies to their foster parents and back to the Home for their "showing" to adoptive parents. Often, she became a foster parent and took care of one or two babies at a time, especially ones with special needs.

It was only because I could live at home, that I could afford college. Dad and I agreed to share the expense. Each quarter, he paid the larger bill of tuition or books and I paid the lesser amount. I was able to take leadership positions, not only was I active in Wesley Foundation, a Methodist College organization, but I was also elected to the Student Senate as a representative of the Independent Student Organization.

My senior year at North Dakota Agricultural College was almost over. I knew my parents would be having many changes in their lives, because the big mansion Home was closing. They were to move in 1957 to their dream place called "The Children's Village." It was located on University Drive near Dakota Clinic. There, Mom, Dad, and Myra would have a new, modern two-bedroom apartment in the basement of one of the three cottages. They were very excited.

As I reflect back, I realize I must have been too immersed in my own plans to appreciate the significance of the closing of our special institution, The North Dakota Children's Home. Actually, in our minds it was not closing, it was just moving into a new setting. When the property was sold to St. Anthony of Padua Church for additional classrooms for their school, few items were salvaged from our old place for keepsakes.

The only item I have from the Home is the original school bell that was rung before each mealtime. The handle is cracked and well worn from all the times it had been rung to bring the children together. As a remembrance of the special holidays, I have purchased a few Fiesta dishes and tumblers for my family gatherings. Now, family meals remind me of the celebrations at the Home.

Just out of college, I left Fargo for my first real job. Now, the Home I had known for 22 years was gone. Along with all the children who had lived there, I had no "Home."

The Home We Shared

Old Children's Home in Fargo to be torn down or moved. (Fargo Forum)

Old Children's Home Here to Be Removed

For its first 58 years, a building at 8th Avenue and 10th Street South in Fargo housed young and helpless children, more than 9,000 of them, orphaned, abandoned or crippled. All were taken in by the former North Dakota Children's Home Society an give attention and love.

Even after the private social agency moved to its present location at 1721 S. University Drive and became known as Children's Village in 1958, the frame structure built in 1897 at 804 10th Street South, continued to shelter children. From then and until last week, it provided school classrooms for St. Anthony of Padua Catholic Church across the avenue to the north.

Children's voices no longer are heard in the two-story structure because the 73-year-old building is slated for demolition. A condominium or apartment complex will rise on the site.

Twin City Construction Co. of Fargo has purchased the property from St. Anthony parish and plans to start construction of the new houses soon after the building is removed.

Albert. P. Smith, executive vice president of the company, said anyone who wants the building, stripped of its movable property, can have it totally free of cost if it is torn down and the lot is cleaned up by March 15.

Permanent equipment includes many old style lighting fixtures, the heating plant and piping, doors, windows and other attached articles, Smith said.

Msgr. Frank J. Nestor, pastor of St. Anthony's, said the parish's extra classroom space needs have been reduced in recent years because of declining school population.

As an example, he said, there were 790 children in 20 classrooms in St. Anthony school in 1957. Now, there are 265.

Through last week, the seven classrooms in the building were being used for religious classes for Catholic children in public schools.

Father Nestor said the school bus garage on the property will be moved to another nearby parish-owned lot.

The Home We Shared

Other Children Share Their Memories Of Our Home

Hazel Baringer Hoeppner

May Berge Bredeson

Margaret Wogh

Florence Wiest Faust

Alton Graf

Rosalie Reis Rosenaw

Royal Wayne Bahr

Dorothy Noell Anderson

Delbert Knowlen

Gloria Wang

Alice Tannehill

Siblings Are Reunited After 48 Years

Meta Mae Madden

The Home We Shared

Hazel Barringer Hoeppner

Erma Hazel Barringer Hoeppner, the daughter of Charles and Annie Graff Barringer, was born July 20, 1906, in Clothe, Minnesota When she was a very young child her left foot was severed in a farm accident. Her mother, Annie, worked quickly and placed her foot into a sack of flour to stop the bleeding, thus saving her life.

The next years, one of her brothers would design from wood blocks, "legs" for her, so that she could walk without a limp. Each year of growth, the brother would add more inches onto the wood creations.

She received her education at Towner, North Dakota, grade school where she lived with and worked for a family. She remembered that a Mrs. McDonald, a Social Worker, came from the NDCH and took her to Fargo. Lucy Hall, a nurse, took care of her when she had Small Pox. Later she received her first artificial foot.

Hazel Barringer after the accident.

She graduated from Fargo Central High School in 1926. Following her high school graduation, she attended Dakota Business College. Now, Hazel, herself, continues her story.

Written by Hazel for the 1991 Reunion

The children in the Home came from all over North Dakota. Mother and Daddy Hall went several hundred miles to bring children to the Home. I remember one family in particular by the name of Layer; whose father had murdered a family named Wolf from Turtle Lake, North Dakota in the 1920s.

The Home was run with money from the people of North Dakota, as well as western Minnesota and surrounding states. Clothing, as well as money, was contributed. I had often wondered if any money was sent from Towner, North Dakota, where I had been for several years. Just this summer (1991), as I went back to visit friends in Towner, I was informed that the school at Towner had given money to the Home while I was there.

Daddy Hall, being a 33rd degree Mason and whose ancestry dated

The Home We Shared

Four Barringer siblings: Art, Vernie, Hazel and Olive, 1918.

back to the Revolutionary War, was a very patriotic man. Many times at our morning devotions, he would have us repeat the American Creed and on Lincoln's Birthday, he always asked me to recite the Gettysburg Address.

In our English classes in high school, we had to learn different poems. When I visited Mother Hall in 1954 at Geneva, Ohio, she asked me if I still remembered the poems I learned in high school. I said, "Perhaps I had forgotten a few," and she said, "You better learn them again." These were some of the teachings that were instilled within me, while at the Home.

Christmas was a very special time for all of us. We always had a tree with gifts for everyone. To make our lives happier, many organizations, such as Kiwanis, Rotary, Eagles, Phythians, Salvation Army, Masons, and many others would bring us fruit, gifts, and candy. Each night after school we could have a treat.

The reason I did not like high school was the fact that in the transfer from Agassiz to Central High School, I found many more students than I was accustomed to. I also thought it was better to earn a living than go to high school. It was then that Mother Hall persuaded me to continue high school.

THE HOME WE SHARED

Left to right: Bob Barringer (Hazel's nephew), Hazel Barringer Hoeppner, and family members, 1978.

Because there were so many different ages of children in the Home, different groups had different times to go to bed. This ranged from 7 o'clock to 8:30 or 9 o'clock which included we older girls, aged 14 to 17. Each group had their own dormitories. The dorm I was in had five beds. These beds always had to be made before going to school.

On Sunday nights, when we were unable to go to church, we gathered around the piano at the Home and Mother Hall, or a member of the working staff, played and we had a "songfest." We were not allowed to play cards, but could play "Flinch" or checkers. We were also allowed to play "fun bingo." On other nights we had to do our homework, which sometimes lasted until bedtime.

While I worked out, the only time I had to study was during study periods at the high school, unless I would stay up real late at night and miss much of my sleep.

During my freshman year, while I worked at the Hutchinsen's, I took Algebra, which was very difficult for me. Mr. and Mrs. Boyden, parents of Mrs. Hutchinson stayed there, also. Grandpa Boyden would help me with my Algebra problems.

After I graduated from high school and business college, I worked in offices for a couple of years. Then the Depression struck and jobs were not plentiful, so I decided to go to Iowa to be with my aunt and uncle and my brother and sisters, who had previously gone there. My uncle ran a livestock business and operated many farms. I helped him in many ways and kept the books for him. I also helped with household duties.

At the Home, our day started at 6 o'clock. There was an average of 28 kids, ranging from babies to 15 or 16 years of age. There was a night nurse on duty during the night and the helpers came on at 6 o'clock; getting the children washed, dressed, and ready for breakfast. The first bell

The Home We Shared

Left to right: Henry Hoeppner (Hazel's husband), Hazel Barringer Hoeppner, Lillian Barringer (Bob Barringer's mother at 90 years), Olive (Hazel's sister) and Betty (Olive's daughter).

rang at quarter to 7, which meant that everyone should gather in the worker's dining room for devotionals headed by Daddy Hall. In case of his absence, a nurse was authorized to take his place for devotions.

After age 14, the older girls were allowed to sit together at a special table in the worker's dining room. The other children went to their tables in the children's dining room. They were taught to say grace before their dinners and suppers and to learn table manners. We always had plenty to eat, and could even have seconds if we cleaned our plates. I remember a certain cereal I did not care for. I went without food for three meals until I finally ate it. We were never allowed to leave the table until everyone was finished or excused by the worker in charge. This discipline was instilled with me the rest of my life.

I was allowed to babysit with several families in Fargo; one being a former Mayor, namely Harry Laskowitz. After I was 14, I was allowed to work for a Fargo family, going at 6 o'clock a.m., returning at 8:30 to go to school at Agassiz, about 10 blocks from where I worked. I changed my clothes at the Home and then went to school.

From the Obituary of Hazel Hoeppner

"Following her schooling, [Hazel Hoeppner] worked in Fargo and Minneapolis, Minnesota, as a bookkeeper at Huber Manufacturing. She moved to Ruthven, Iowa, in 1932 and has lived in Spencer, Iowa, since 1948.

The Home We Shared

On January 6, 1976, she married Henry Hoeppner in Mayflower, Arkansas. Following their marriage they lived in Spencer. While living in Spencer, she was a member of the First Baptist Church and the American Legion Auxiliary. She also enjoyed knitting and putting together puzzles. On Tuesday, October 7, 1997, Mrs. Hoeppner passed away at the St. Luke Lutheran Home in Spencer, Iowa, at the age of 91. She was preceded in death by her parents; her husband on August 3, 1992; seven brothers and four sisters. She is survived by three sisters-in-law, as well, as many nieces and nephews.

(Hazel's nephew, Bob Barringer, and his wife, Delores, of Spencer, Iowa, provided Hazel's information and story.)

The Home We Shared

A Letter from May Berge Bredeson
September 24, 2003

Dear Dorothy,

In spite of the 13 years difference in our ages, we seem to have quite a lot in common. My memories of the North Dakota Children's Home go back to before you were born. I remember eating a meal at the Home once with my girlfriend, Irene Roach. Irene's mother, who was an acquaintance of my mother, worked at the Home. I don't recall what we ate, except that one of the girls who lived there didn't like the sauce served. She put it in her pocket and dumped it on the playground when we went outside. This would have been in 1929, as I recall that Irene and I, at that same time had instigated a 10th Anniversary Party for my parents.

Since my home was midway between the Crittenton Home and the Children's Home, I remember seeing the expectant mothers out walking to get their exercise and many children from the Home coming and going to Agassiz Junior High School.

There was another way that I learned more about the children from the Home. My mother had good friends on a farm by Butte, North Dakota. The couple, John and Caroline Dalos, were foster parents to many children from the Home.

One foster girl, Evelyn, stayed with them many years. Evelyn was a few years younger than Clara, the Dalos' daughter. Two boys were Norman Cross and Joe Jacklin. One summer I visited the Dalos farm and remember playing with Joe. He captured a bunny for me; but, by the time we were ready to leave the farm, it had escaped, much to his dismay.

I recently contacted Roland Haugen, who was a neighbor to the Dalos family, years ago. They stated that Norman Cross was there only for a short time. Norm must have been placed on a farm nearby, as they remember he came by horseback to visit with the Dalos family.

Later, there were two young men, Victor Rollette and Robert Peterson, who came to the farm. Later, they moved with Mr. and Mrs. Dalos when they retired from the farm and went to live at Auburn, Washington, to be near their daughter, Clara.

John and Caroline Dalos, November, 1949. Foster parents to many children.

The Home We Shared

My friend, John, remembers Victor as being very creative. Near the house, he made a rather large fishpond for gold fish and it was complete with a Dutch windmill to circulate the water for the fish. Victor also made several sleds and a nice wooden bi-plane for Roland. After moving to Washington, Victor returned to North Dakota at least one time to visit.

Robert returns frequently and most recently for the Butte Church 100th Anniversary in 2001. Robert and his wife are in the photo taken at the church at that event.

Robert Peterson and his wife, taken at the Butte Church 100th Anniversary, 2001.

I am sure the children were expected to work on the Dalos farm, but from my observation John and Caroline were good people and treated the children well. For instance, when my mother and I stayed there, Caroline would come in our bedroom first thing in the morning with a sip of wine and a cookie to start the day.

Best Wishes,
May Berge Bredeson

The Home We Shared

Margaret Wogh Shares Her Story
By Margaret and Ann Wogh

I was born in Slope County, North Dakota, on June 16, 1926, on a farm near Amidon. I contracted Polio when I was two years old. My parents were devastated. They had to find help as soon as possible.

They were referred to Mr. Harold Bond. He made arrangements to take me to the Children's Home in Fargo. I received medical attention from the doctors in Fargo and Dr. Emil Geist, an orthopedic surgeon of Minneapolis.

Margaret, four years old, and Mary Leazer with the St. Anthony Church and School in the background, 1930.

Jean Love, a caseworker for many years wrote this note in 1978.

"Part of the time during Margaret Wogh's care, she was cared for by a wealthy Minneapolis family, who became so attached to her they wanted to adopt her. Margaret's parents were unwilling to give her up for adoption. Margaret was a great favorite with everyone at the Home."

My family moved to another farm near Belfield, North Dakota. When I was six years old, I came home for visits and to heal from the surgery I had on my right ankle. My first year of school, I had a tutor at my home, as I wasn't able to go to school.

Then, when I was 10 years old, I

Margaret exercising her ankles.

The Home We Shared

Margaret, class of 1946.

Margaret, 1963.

Margaret, right, with her sister, Ann, outside their California home, 1990s.

returned to the Home for more medical care. I remember more about this second time at the Home. We always had to clean up our plates at meal times and share in chores. Many persons took care of me, but the workers I remember are Mr. and Mrs. Harold Bond, Mr. and Mrs. Amil Lund, Mrs. Layborne, and Mrs. Raines.

My mother was very concerned about my schooling. Since we are a Catholic family, the staff at the Home made arrangements for me to attend St. Anthony School across the street from the Home. I liked school and the nuns were very good to me.

Christmas was always nice and exciting. We received gifts of clothes and toys. Also, summers were special, as during these two

The Home We Shared

years I was able to go to the lake in Minnesota. Living at the Children's Home helped me to grow up and be independent.

At age 12, I returned to my family. I rode the train alone to Belfield, which is west of Dickinson. There my family picked me up at the train station and took me back to our farm home.

In 1944, my parents decided to move to Petaluma, California I was 17 years old. Two years later, I finished High School in Petaluma.

I had surgery on both knees at the Children's Hospital in San Francisco. My sister, Ann, was working in San Francisco so I stayed with her when I had treatments on my legs. We were living close to the Children's Hospital, thus I walked two blocks to the hospital everyday for six weeks. Then, I went home to recuperate.

Later I returned to San Francisco to work. I was employed as an Insurance Clerk for 30 years. I enjoyed living in San Francisco very much. There was a lot to do — go to the park, zoo, movies and shows. San Francisco is 50 miles south of Petaluma. Often, Ann and I would go home on weekends.

When Ann and I decided to retire, we acquired a home north of San Francisco where we took care of our elderly mother. Mom was from a large family and they held many reunions with over 80 to 100 relatives and friends attending.

We continue to enjoy our lives here in California. We always have a lot to do. I appreciate my sister, Ann, who assisted me in writing this story.

The Home We Shared

Florence Wiest Faust, Child Photographer

One Christmas, while Florence Wiest was a resident at the Home, she attended the Lions Christmas party. Her special gift was a Brownie camera that she immediately put to good use. Many of her photos are shared in her story.

Florence was 12 years old when she arrived at the Home (around 1935) with her eight-year-old brother, Floyd, and 10-year-old sister, Gladys. Both of their parents had died and no relatives were able to take them into their homes. Florence remembers that very few of the children at the Home were actually "orphans."

Florence Wiest in front of her Home, 1936.

Gladys Wiest by the steps of the playroom, 1936.

The Home We Shared

Within a few months, relatives took in her brother and sister, but Florence remained at the Home for three years while attending Agassiz Junior High School. Florence can "map out" the Home in her mind. She sees the children's dining room with the door at the end of the room to the Lund's apartment. She wonders, "Where were you, Dorothy, when your parents worked?"

She moves through the Home to the steps leading to the second floor through the staff dining room. She tells of the large bathroom at the top of the steps and remembers how the new children received their first bath at the Home. "Their old clothes were taken away and burned. Then, the new, clean clothes were given to them."

She recalls the children each having their own peg on the bathroom wall, where they would hang their personal towel and washcloth.

Florence thinks the library was off limits to the children, as it was used by the caseworkers for showing children. But, she tells of a huge dollhouse in there with even a little greenhouse on the top floor.

Most of Florence's hours at the Home were spent helping in the playroom or in the nursery. She loved taking care of the babies. On one election year, she believes, "Mr. Bond asked the workers to vote a certain way or lose their jobs."

Some of the boys. Back row: Edward and Harold. Middle row: Rondo, floyd, Vern, LeRoy and George. Front row: Billy, Billy, Nickie and Freddie.

How she loved to take pictures. Her personal album is full of children's faces, but not always a name to go with them. The older children loved to go to the "Five and Dime," to have their pictures taken in an automatic photo booth. Sometimes two or three would try to fill the booth for the photo. As she talks, suddenly, some of the children's names begin to flow, and she wonders what happened to them. One person she remembers well is Meta Mae Madden. She also thinks about

The Home We Shared

The Weist children "at play."

Frankie, a crippled boy.

One time, Florence had new shoes and they wore a blister on her heel. She remembers telling the nurse, Mrs. Larson, that it hurt. It was ignored until Florence had blood poisoning. Then, Mrs. Larson spent many hours taking care of her with hot compresses.

Sometimes the Home children would stand on their side of the street and taunt the Catholic schoolchildren with a "Cat-lickers" chant. To which the schoolchildren responded with "Pros-stinkers." Snowballs were sometimes lobbed across the street at each other.

During her three years of high school, Florence lived with the Lester Rohde Family. He owned the Rohde Candy Company. She took care of their two daughters and each summer, they took her to their lake cottage on Pelican Lake.

Florence attended Fargo Central High School, graduating in 1943. She is not sure who paid for her school expenses. She had very few clothes. She attended high school interchanging two skirts, three blouses, and two cotton dresses. She is anxiously looking forward to the next school reunion to be held in Fargo.

One time Mrs. Rohde was concerned about Florence's winter coat and sent her with a credit card to the department store. When Florence returned with a tan, camelhair coat with a zip-out lining, Mrs. Rohde began to cry. Florence thinks it was because she had not purchased a more expensive coat; but this coat was so practical. She could wear it many seasons due to the zip-out lining.

For six years, the Methodist Youth Fellowship at First Methodist Church offered Florence many hours of fun and spiritual growth. It was here that she met her future husband, Charles Faust. They married in 1945 at Portland, Oregon. They continued to live there and raised their family of five. Lucia, born in 1946, presently lives in Minnesota. Charles,

The Home We Shared

The Home through the eyes of Florence's Brownie camera.

"Hansie," our cook and Mrs. Laybourne, our "right hand lady," 1937.

born in 1948, died on June 13, 2003, at age 54. Jeffrey was born in 1950 and is Superintendent of Schools in Eugene, Oregon. Judy was born in 1952 and died in 1956 at the age of three years. Wayne was born in 1954 and turns 50 in 2004. Charles, the husband of Florence, died May 26, 1967, at age 50, leaving her to take full responsibility for this large family.

Years later, she learned that her sister, Gladys, was diagnosed with tuberculosis, sent to the Sanitarium at Dunseith, North Dakota, and died there in 1943. Her brother, Floyd, lived with relatives. He worked very hard on their farm in the fields and cleaning the barn. After

Florence's graduation picture, 1943.

finishing high school, he went into the service, later married, and raised a family.

Florence recalls the following workers at the Home: Mrs. Laybourne, a red-headed person; Mrs. Larson, the nurse; Mrs. Raines; Miss Marietta Hanson, the cook; Mr. Bond, superintendent; and the Lund family.

She mentioned that she did not see Dorothy much as a very small child. Mrs. Cook, a neighbor lady, must have taken care of her.

As she looks back, she felt good about living at the Home. She writes, "I had a home and no people who disliked us." She continues, "I was well taken care of."

The Home We Shared

Alton Graf

In 1999, I presented the "Orphan Train Riders" program at the Public Library at Bismarck, North Dakota. I closed with the slides of the North Dakota Children's Home and two slides of my parent's wedding. A gentleman in the audience said, "I was at that wedding. I was five years old and living at the Home."

What an exciting event. I had never met a child from the Home who had attended the wedding. Now, Alton tells his story.

Elise Alton and family, 1928.

Alton and Tommy at the Home.

My birth mother's name was Elise Alton, but I never heard why my siblings and I had to be placed in the Children's Home. I was between three and four years old when I arrived at the Home with my three sisters and two brothers. I had another older brother, but he ran away before we were delivered to the Home.

For a while I was hospitalized. I do not know at which hospital or for what reason. At the Home, I recall the food was good, but I did not like squash! Thank goodness, we usually only had it in the fall.

Some of the workers I remember, were Mr. Bond, Mr. Lund, Miss Leazer, and Miss Wells. They taught us to behave, but at the same time they were kind to us. We had good clothes and lots of toys. I was too young to work. I remember going to the lake

The Home We Shared

Mom Graf and Alton, 1940.

Fred and Katie Graf, 1930s.
Alton's adoptive parents.

in the summer!

We had many parties. Some were Christmas, 4th of July, Halloween, and Thanksgiving. Another great party was the wedding of Mr. Lund and Miss Leazer. We children were all dressed up in our best clothes. I think the wedding took place in the parlor of the Children's Home (this was most likely the Staff Dining Room). It was a special day for all of us.

I remember going to church and Sunday school. When I was five I went to kindergarten and then I attended a half year of first grade. In January of 1932, I left the Home at age six. Miss Wells, a red-haired lady, and I rode the train to Mandan, North Dakota, where my new dad and mom, Fred and Katie Graf, met us. I remember the year, as I turned seven in March at my new home.

Lorraine and Alton, 1982.

The Home We Shared

Within the year they adopted me and I was named, Alton Graf. I took my original family last name as my first name.

We lived on a farm eight miles west of New Salem, North Dakota. Living on the Graf farm made a farmer, rancher, and part-time miner out of me. My Dad had a coal mine on his land. He leased it to one of the guys that used to work for him. When I was older, I got to drive the truck for the coal mine. I liked that better than farming, but I have no regrets as to being brought up on the farm.

I continued to live with Mom and Dad Graf until they passed away. Dad died in 1976 and Mom died in 1979. In July of 1982, I married Lorraine Goldade, who is the best little woman and takes good care of me. We have had our hardships and sorrows, but married life is better than being single!

The Home We Shared

Rosalie, A True Survivor
Written by Rosalie Reis Rosenaw

I, Rosalie Reis Rosenaw, was one of nine children, five boys and four girls, raised by our parents, John and Eva Reis, on our farm near Linton, North Dakota.

When I was only one year and seven months old, I became ill with Polio. It left me with crippled ankles and feet, which the doctors called "flop ankles." From that time on, I was not able to walk.

When I was seven to nine years old, the county nurse took me yearly to the St. Paul Children's Hospital. Each time I traveled to the hospital, the doctors would fuse bones to my ankles, working on one ankle at a time. They did this to make the ankles stiff and strong. After these many surgeries, I was able to walk fairly well. But, of course, I never had a natural walk. I was labeled "crippled."

I attended the country school, but was not able to play games like the other children. One winter, while attending the school, I froze my feet, as many days the teacher would not build a fire in the stove.

A "Five and Dime" photo of Rosalie.

Because of my feet freezing, my incisions opened and started to drain. My parents drove me to the doctor at Linton. Right away, the doctor asked the county nurse to take me to St. John's Hospital in Fargo, North Dakota. My parents didn't have the money to make the trip, nor could Dad drive in the big cities.

From the years I was 13 to 20, I would continue to go to St. John's Hospital to have more surgeries on my ankles and to allow time in between for them to heal. Those years, I would leave my parents and siblings the first days of March and travel to Fargo. I would often return in October or November. I had 19 surgeries throughout those years.

When I was in Fargo, I would spend about seven to eight weeks in the hospital. Then, I would go to the North Dakota Children's Home for recovery. It was less expensive to stay there.

Every day at the Home, Mr. Bond would take me to the hospital for Therapy Treatments. At that time I was either in a wheelchair or on crutches.

The Home We Shared

Rosalie from Florence Weist's collection, 14 years old.

Many times, Mr. and Mrs. Bond would have me to their house for meals. They lived across the alley behind the Home. Mrs. Bond would have the table set for a king! The Bonds were such nice people.

I enjoyed my many months at the Home. The girls and boys had lots of fun playing games. During the summers, the crippled children came from all over the state. Once, while we played, a young fellow and I made believe we were getting married. The rest of the kids attended the "wedding."

Another time, coming from the hospital, my incisions had not healed. I wore casts that could be removed for therapy and treatments to the wounds to assist with the healing. It had rained very hard that night and the next day I was out playing with the other kids. My incisions were itching, so I took one cast off and laid my foot in the cold, muddy water. From that escapade, I became sick with blood poisoning.

They took me to the hospital where I went into a coma and almost died. Some of the children from the Home came every day and prayed for me by my bedside. When I came out of the coma, the doctors, nurses, and children cried.

I remember getting into trouble another time. At night, all of the crippled children had to be carried up the long flight of stairs to the second floor for baths and to sleep. Then, in the morning each one was carried down for their meals, treatments, and playtimes.

One morning, I decided not to wait for Mr. Bond or the other man that carried each child downstairs. I started down on my bottom with my feet and legs extended in front of me. Bumpity, bump.... I proceeded down each step. Soon, Mrs. Laybourne and Mr. Bond found me on the steps and scolded me soundly. I never did that again!

When I was 24 years of age, I married Albert Rosenaw. We have a daughter, Dianna. Now, she is married to Allan Zerr and they have two children. They visit me often.

My siblings have always been supportive of me. We are a very close

Rosalie Reis Rosenaw, circa 1990s.

family and help each other through the good and bad times. In 2000, we experienced the death of one of my sisters. We gathered to grieve over her loss and assisted her husband for many months following her death.

Now, as I write this in 2003, a brother has had a stroke. Again, the family members have gathered in Portland to assist him.

Since 1993, I am having what is called "Post Polio." From the onset, I decided not to travel by wheelchair, so I am still walking. My feet are very weak as the nerves and muscles are fading away. I had to give up driving (boo hoo!) and now use a walker when I go outside.

In all these years, I have had 35 surgeries. You see God loves me and picked me to be the one to go through the suffering. With His guidance and help from the many special people, who have cared for me through these years; I am thankful that I have lived an active life.

With love,
Rosalie

The Home We Shared

Retired Sergeant Major Royal W. Bahr
"Reporting In"
By Royal Bahr

My name is Royal Wayne Bahr. I first came to the North Dakota Children's Home, located at 804 10th Street South, Fargo, North Dakota, sometime before the end of 1936. I was just under six years of age.

The first time you saw the Home, you would have had to be impressed by the size of the main building. The Home and two other buildings occupied half of a city block.

Royal Bahr

When you came upon the front entrance, you would notice a long porch that runs from one end of the building to the other end. When you entered the front door, the first thing you would notice was the wide staircase that leads to the second floor.

On the first floor as you enter, was the office of Mr. Harold Bond, Superintendent of the Home. To the left side was the library, where I spent a lot of time. The dining room for the staff sat off to the left of the staircase with the kitchen behind the staff dining room. As you went past the staircase, on the right was the children's dining room, large enough to seat all of the children at one time.

Off to the right of this dining room was an area where the annual Christmas trees were set up. There was another narrow area off to the right where a clothes chute was located for sending clothes down to the laundry. To the left and rear of the dining room was a door that led to the quarters of the custodian, Mr. Amil Lund. His wife, Mary, and daughter, Dorothy, lived there, also.

As you go back to the staircase and up to the second floor, you would find the sleeping areas for all the children. The boys slept in a large dormitory with a cot or bunk bed for each boy. To the rear was a nursery. The girls slept in several different rooms according to their ages.

There was a very large basement in the Home that was used for many purposes. It contained a furnace, hot water heater, and storage rooms, as well as a coal chute. There was a large area for the children to play in during inclement weather. In addition, there was a laundry room and an ironing room. I spent some time in there during one of my punishment terms.

The Home We Shared

Brigadier General Maurice D. Edwards, Deputy Commander of Fort Jackson (on left) presents the "Best Area-Coordinators Award" to Sergeant Major, Royal Bahr (on right). Royal's wife, Joy, is looking on.

As you leave the Home from the rear, you will see two other buildings: one is a cottage in which nurses and other staff members slept. I slept in one of those rooms on one of my returns to the Home. The other building was a large garage. As I said before, the Home occupied half a city block and the rest of the property was a large field or playground. I spent a lot of time on the field playing football, soccer, baseball, and softball. I even broke a rib playing football!

The reason I came to the Home was because my father died in 1934. After his death, my mother had a nervous breakdown and was sent to a mental institution located at Grafton, North Dakota. I had one brother and three sisters. The children were split up and went in different directions. My cousin, George Bahr, had me for a while and then I was placed in the Home.

I really don't remember anything prior to first grade. The children at the Home went to Hawthorne Elementary School, a distance of about six blocks. We had to travel that distance four times a day, as there were no school lunches available during this period of time. At school, I remember the refreshment breaks consisting of milk and cookies.

During recess, we normally played soccer or tag. Some of the boys' names were Theodore (Teddy) Baer, Tom Mikelson, Buddy Swartz and the Maris boys, Rudy and Roger (yes, the baseball hero). Rudy and Roger

The Home We Shared

left to go to Sacred Heart, later renamed Shanley High School, where Roger developed his athletic skills.

After the first grade, I was placed in the foster home of Christ Larson and family. With me were my brother, Orville, and sister, Delores. Mr. Larson lived in the Fort Ransom area and there I went to a rural school and passed the second grade. Later, my Aunt Helen got custody of me, and I moved in with her at Mandan.

While I was in Mandan, I lived with another cousin, who was separated from her husband, but had custody of their daughter, Audrey. I played with the neighborhood children and went to a Catholic school.

After school I liked to play and explore the caves around Mandan and the Missouri River. It was during one of these excursions that I hurt my right ankle. When I took off my boot, a spider fell out. My ankle was wrapped and I went to school the next day. My ankle was still sore and I couldn't put it under my desk and a boy stepped on it.

Barry, a graduate of the Citadel, oldest son of Royal and Joy Bahr.

Now, it was really sore and I was mad at the boy; so during recess, I pushed him into a swing set. I felt good about that, but the priest took exception and wanted me to come to church and make a confession. I never showed, because I was put in a hospital in Mandan and later transferred to St. Luke's Hospital in Fargo, North Dakota. Dr. Joel Swanson operated on my ankle. My injury was diagnosed as osteomyelitis — an infection of the marrow of the bone. It was probably caused by the bite from the spider, which may have been a Brown Recluse.

After I was pronounced, "ready to leave the hospital," I was once again placed in the Children's Home. I could have gone to the Crippled Children's Home, but since I had been at the Children's Home before, they decided to put me back into the Children's Home.

Since I hadn't completed the third grade in Mandan, I started it all over again at Hawthorne where I completed the third and fourth grades. I was halfway through the fifth grade when I was sent to live with my cousin, George Bahr, again. I still don't know why they didn't wait until the end of the school year.

The time during which I was at the Children's Home was an enjoyable experience, at least most of the time. At first it was hard because I had to walk the six blocks to school on crutches. I was picked on by some of the bullies at the Home and at school, but not for long. They soon realized that I would fight back! At the Home, Mr. Bond put the bullies in

The Home We Shared

their place by threatening to send them to the Training School at Mandan. At school, I met some of my friends I had known in the first grade, who stood up for me. After I got off the crutches, I was able to participate in athletics again.

The most enjoyable time at the Home was the summer vacations spent at Pelican Lake in Minnesota. We lived in a big log cabin owned by the Episcopal Church called, Holiday House. The kitchen, dining room and some type of living room were on the first floor. I don't know where the girls slept, but the boys slept upstairs in double-decker bunks or in a large dormitory on cots.

Our daily routine included going for a swim before breakfast, in other words, if you wanted to eat, you had to take a dip! We also had to take a nap after our noon lunch. We went on numerous nature hikes, led by Mr. Lund. He took us on boat trips across the lake. We got to ride on a motor launch owned by one of our neighbors. The only bad thing that happened during my last summer at the lake was when a girl accused me of molesting her and I got punished. She lied and I don't know why.

As much as I enjoyed the summers, I actually enjoyed all seasons, especially the Toboggan Runs at Island Park in Fargo. I was a pretty mischievous youngster, and with some other kids, got into a lot of trouble: snowballing the "cat-lickers" (Catholic children) at St. Anthony School across the street; breaking into vacant houses or maybe even houses that were occupied; visiting haunted houses including Dill Hill, a vacant college. I ran away from the Home twice, once splitting my head on a 4x4 under the Home. Dr. John Bond fixed me up, so I could go to school.

I made one more trip back to the Home in 1942. I had stepped on a nail at a grain elevator site and my cousin, George, brought me back to Fargo for treatment. I was on a pair of crutches again and a boy came up to me and said, "I don't like cripples."

Another boy came up to him and said, "That's no cripple, he's Royal Bahr." Just like I was some legend.

If there were one thing unfavorable about the Home, I would have to say that it would be their habit of sending children to foster homes that were farms. There, many children became nothing more than a hired hand. I say this because I experienced it. Several years ago on one of my trips to North Dakota, my cousin, George, and his wife, Gustie, apologized to me for their treatment.

Valley City College High was where I was able to attend school for three years and graduated in 1951. I lettered in track for two years and worked after school, weekends and evenings at Dakota Drug Store during those years.

From November, '51 to '52, I worked at the Black Hills Ordnance Depot, Igloo, SD. It was the same place Tom Brokaw's father worked about seven years earlier. From there, I was drafted into the Army on November 18, 1952. After Basic-Advanced Training, I was sent to Japan

The Home We Shared

for the rest of my tour of Duty, got out for 81 days, re-enlisted in January, '55, and stayed in until March of '83. I retired as a Sergeant Major.

I met Joy Kiyoe in March of 1959, and married her during my second Tour of Duty in Japan. This union produced four children and six grandchildren. The oldest son, Barry, and his wife, Ruth, have two children Coleman and Alyssa. Linda, our oldest daughter, is still looking for "Mr. Right." Teresa, the youngest daughter, is married to Scott Beals and they have two children, Erika and Keenan. Grover, our youngest son, and wife, Paulette, have two daughters Katelyn and Kassidy. My beautiful wife, Joy, passed away September, 1997, at the age of 62.

Going back to my Army life, some of my more interesting jobs were a tour of Duty in Vietnam in 1967 and becoming First Sergeant in the First Infantry Division in Germany, 1972-1974. Then, I became Chief Instructor and later Sergeant Major of the Army Administration School, in Fort Jackson, SC.

Finally, I ended my career in the Army with a four-year tour as an Enlisted Commander (one of five to hold this job). I worked with the

Left to right: Ruth (Barry's wife), Barry, Linda (second child of Royal and Joy), Royal, Scott (Teresa's husband), Teresa (third child of Royal and Joy), and Joy. Only Grover is missing from the photo.

The Home We Shared

Defense Investigative Services, Military Intelligence Units, and Military Entrance Stations going from one major city to another including the country of Puerto Rico.

To complete my government service, I worked for the United States Postal Service for 13 years, a total of 44 years of Government Service.

Grover Bahr, youngest child, with Royal and Joy Bahr.

THE HOME WE SHARED

DOROTHY NOELL ANDERSON RECEIVES "DAY CARE"

Three Dorothy's and Mary at Camp Watson.

"Dottie" came to the Home each day that her mother worked. She became an extension of the Lund family. My mother, Mary, had taken on the responsibility of this child. Because I was 12 years old, I was asked to watch over "Dottie" and Myra, when I was home from school.

Dottie lived with her mother, Dorothy, Grandpa Otto Luther, and two Great Aunts about 10 blocks from the Home. When Dottie was about two, her birth father had deserted them. Thus, her mother had to earn a living. Her father and aunts were elderly, so her mother asked for daycare at the Home.

Dottie and her Mother, Dorothy,, 1944.

Part of taking care of Dottie led us into being part of their family, too. Many visits and Christmases were spent at the Luther house. My father, Amil, was on hand to take pictures and we watched this child growing up before our eyes.

Her mother married a young, service man, Arthur Noell, and the two Dorothy's moved away with him to North Carolina. Dorothy and Arthur had two more children, eight and 17 years younger than Dottie.

Even though they had left our lives, my family continued to write to their family throughout the years. Also, the Lunds took on special cares and visits with the elderly Luther relatives until their deaths.

Dottie married Jim Anderson and they have three daughters.

Their oldest daughter, Beth, and husband, Anthony Armstrong, have three children, Jack, six years; Ellie, four years; and Ivy, six months old. Anthony participated in the December, 2003, New Zealand triathlon. He placed 45th in the World in the age division for 35 year olds.

Dottie and Jim's middle daughter, Fran, and husband, Lou McMeekin, have recently had their first child, Lillian. Their youngest daughter, Jan, is six feet tall and does some modeling. She works in Charlotte, NC.

Dottie is an example of another type of service given by the Home to children. It was special to have her and her family involved in our lives.

Myra, dottie and Dorothy, 1949.

Dottie, Grandpa Mr. Luther, Aurthur and Dorothy, 1949.

Arhtur and Dorothy Nell, 1949.

The Home We Shared

Delbert Knowlen
By Delbert as Told To His Daughter, Marsha

Delbert Knowlen, 1950s.

For five years after my father died, my mother tried to raise us seven children, but soon realized she could not handle the huge task. Thus, it was in 1952 that all of us children were removed from our home.

I was 12 years old and remember a policewoman from Bismarck driving my younger brother, John, my twin sister, Grace, and me, to Fargo to the Children's Home. All of our other siblings were scattered across North Dakota.

I really liked the Home. I felt I was treated well and everyone was good to me. I had clean clothes and many toys to play with. We were disciplined well, just like any other children.

Some of the workers I remember are Mrs. Von Hagen, Mrs. Waterfal, and Mr. Lund, who took me to the lake. I remember his daughters, Dorothy and Myra.

I don't think that I was ever very ill. I do not remember having to work. I was fed very well and sure liked the food.

I liked the school I went to, they taught me very well. I wasn't treated badly by other students or teachers. I remember attending church right at the Home.

I only lived at the home for six months and then I was placed in one foster home where I was abused. Then, when I was 13 years old, I was moved to the home of Howard and Mildred Robinson at Stirrum, North Dakota. I remained in their Christian, caring home until I was 17. In September of 1957, I went to Wahpeton.

Though Mom and Dad Robinson — they were my parents. Even my daughter, — parents."

A sad part of my childhood was — siblings. The older children had gone — at the Home were eventually placed — only my youngest brother, John, was adopted —

[handwritten note: Really good people — he was lucky.]

In 1958, most of my siblings were able to locate each other and from then on we have continued to be in contact with each other by letter or phone calls.

Being placed in the Home gave me a better chance at a good life for my family and myself. My second foster family was a very loving Christian home and they taught me how to give to my own children what they needed to have a successful life. Thus, when there came a time that I couldn't give my own children what they needed, I knew to place them in foster care. That way, they could obtain the best for themselves.

Delbert Knowlen

Delbert Knowlen, 1990s.

The Home We Shared

Gloria Wang: Remembering With Love
By Jennifer Radack

Reprinted from the Centennial Edition of "The Village Crier," Vol. 19, No. 1 — November, 1991.

Gloria Wang

She's handed the photograph. It's an old black and white 5x7 of the North Dakota Children's Home in Fargo, 1902. To me the picture is eerie, an old white orphanage which looks cold and empty. The picture lacks trees, or shrubs, or life. There's no white picket fence. My imagination colors the photo with what I imagine on the inside. The bareness. The isolation. The lack of love. Little Orphan Annie scrubbing floors, face wet with tears.

I watch the photo tremble between her fingers. My eyes trace her figure, skimming until I reach her lips, see her teeth, biting down, trying to stop the quiver. A tear falls and I suddenly feel guilty for forcing these memories on her. I nervously look at her husband sitting slouching in the chair across from me. He wrestles an old handkerchief from his pocket; lint coming with and falling slowly to the floor. He wipes his nose.

"This sure does bring back a lot of memories," she whispers.

Gloria Wang lived in the Fargo Children's Home from 1944 to 1949. She was a wide-eyed child of thirteen when she was brought there, a woman of eighteen when she left. She and her six brothers and sisters were brought to the orphanage several years after her mother died during childbirth. In between the tragic death and the orphanage, Gloria was passed back and forth between foster homes.

"We went to bad homes; they were very mean. Would give us kids lickin's. Didn't like us." She shrugs her shoulders. "I suppose they took us in for the money." She recalls one evening in particular. "I was whipped so bad that I ran to the neighbors. I told them that he was beating us up. They must have called the Welfare office because two weeks later the State came and took us."

She's watching her fingers chase each other, little churchgoers in her hand-made steeple. "Here's the church, here's the steeple." I sing inside my head a rhyme my mother taught me when I was young. Who taught Gloria rhymes? "I didn't go to school after eighth grade. They didn't make me, because I had a speech problem."

She talks with an occasional stutter and minor enunciation problems.

The Home We Shared

I have no trouble understanding her and think it's sad that she didn't get help from a speech pathologist, work on her confidence and continue her education. Yet as I talk more with her, I slowly get the feeling that Gloria doesn't need or want people feeling sorry for her.

I glance at my list of prepared questions and instead see the little house I grew up in. I see myself as a little girl in cut-off shorts and bare feet, chasing my brother through the yard with a green plastic pail full of water from the sprinkler. We're both laughing, showing off our popsicle-stained teeth. Realizing how absurd my questions were I turn to a blank page and ask her to talk in general about the whole experience of being in the orphanage.

"I enjoyed it. I don't know what would've happened if I hadn't been brought to the orphanage. I don't think I would've made it."

She tells me they tried to make it as much like a real home as possible. They all had chores to do (make their bed, clean their room, set the table), three meals a day plus an afternoon snack, curfews (in by 10 o'clock p.m.), house rules and allowances.

"Birthdays were real special. We didn't have to do no chores. And we got a special meal, whatever we wanted. They gave us presents, too. And, we got to sleep in late that day (usual wake-up call being 7:30 a.m.)."

She smiles as she reminisces. "Christmases were always special, very, very special. The Legion and Lion Clubs would buy us all a new outfit of our own. They'd give us presents, like a pass to the movies. And, they'd take us all out to dinner and drive us around town (to see the Christmas lights). Yes, Christmas was a very special time."

Among other chores, Gloria mainly helped take care of the infants and toddlers because she was older. "I loved working with the babies. I had a daycare at my house until just last year (1990). It's what I've done all my life, taking care of babies."

She says that some of the toddlers would get attached to her and call her "mom." "I'd have to correct them, I'd say: 'No mom. My name is Gloria.'"

She says it was always sad to see the babies go, because you spent all your time taking care of them. But, it was nothing compared to the pain of when her sisters got adopted. "They (houseparents) told me that they had to take them to the hospital, to get their tonsils out. They never came back." She shakes her head in silence. "I knew..., I knew...." Finally a few days later I asked and they told me a family adopted them. What hurt was I never got to say, 'good-bye.' They were just gone."

Watching people come and go was a way of life for Gloria. "No one wanted me, I was fat and clumsy and had a speech defect. And I was older, no one wants an older child." When Gloria got sad about the rejection, she went to the housemother. "She'd always tell me that they needed me more at the orphanage. That the little kids needed me. That always made me feel better."

The Home We Shared

Although not allowed to go off the premises after 6 o'clock p.m., she says they were just like normal kids. They'd go for bike rides, go get ice cream, go to movies, play ball in the yard and get in trouble. She laughs as she tells me one vivid memory. "It was Saturday night. We told Mr. Bond (the House Father at the time) that we were going to take the bus into town to go to church. We got off the bus and went over to the Red Apple Café and ate hamburgers and malts. I'll never forget that meal. And then, Mr. Bond comes walking in. He looks at us and says, "Hello, girls." And that's all. The next day he called us into his office and made us take a toothbrush and a bucket of water and scrub the family room." She laughs, "I'll never forget it!"

She reminisces with me for over an hour, all the while my picture of cold cement floors and sadness being slowly shredded to pieces. "I felt loved there. They were good to us: no beatings, and lots of good food to eat. We had singing times, fellowship and story times. The orphanage gave me guidelines to live by."

As they leave my office, Gloria's husband grabs my arm. "Thank You, thank you! This was very interesting; I learned a lot." He glances at his wife. "I've never heard these stories before."

"You don't talk about this kind of stuff," she told me earlier when I asked if people treated her differently for growing up in the Home. "If people find out, they say, 'Who you? You were an orphan?'" As I watch him put his hand on her back and escort her out I wonder if I helped by giving her an opportunity to speak.

The interview is over and I'm driving home. Gloria's ghost seems to be sitting in my passenger seat replaying part of the interview. "I can't bear to see kids mean to their mothers." She shakes her head in sadness.

"Tell me why?" Her eyes search me for an answer. All I could do is shake my head along with her as I relive my own adolescent fights.

Gloria's ghost starts repeating "Tell me why. I never did have a mom," as I drive down 13th Avenue.

The Home We Shared

Alice Tannehill

To obtain Alice Tannehill's story for this book, I called her at her home. While visiting over the phone with Alice, she reminded me of the many hours we had spent together in the Home library. We not only studied for school but, also, for confirmation and Sunday school. She remembers that we had to learn the Beatitudes by memory. We had an extremely active Junior High Methodist Youth Fellowship to be involved in each week. Alice and I went to camp one summer. She tells the story of looking down the path and seeing another camper coming towards her that looked very much like herself. As they came closer to each other, they realized they were sisters that had been separated after living at the Home. It was her sister, Betty. Different families had adopted each of them.

Alice and I were close friends through Junior High. When she was starting ninth grade, she moved to Bismarck with her adoptive family and graduated from Bismarck High School. We kept in touch through letters.

Our last meeting was in 1954 at Macalester College in St. Paul, Minnesota We had the weekend together, while she showed me around her college campus. Since then, the once-a-year Christmas letters have told of the happenings in each of our families. Every five years or so, a phone call was made between the two of us. But, even for all these contacts, I never

Betty and Alice meet at camp.

Alice Tannehill, 1951, Bismarck High School graduation.

The Home We Shared

knew the story about her birth siblings and why they came to the Home, until this 2004 phone call.

Alice said that the seven siblings had the same mother, but the first two had a different father than the last five. Now, they are learning that the five younger ones are having difficulty with diabetes. Thus, they feel that they received this health problem from their father's side of the family.

Their mother had died in childbirth when Evelyn was born. The oldest child, Hazel or Halo, took the responsibility at age 16 to write a letter to Lucy Hall at the Home to explain the plight of her siblings. It was then that all but Halo were gathered up and taken to the Home. Halo went to Grand Forks to work in a Nursing Home until she was 18 year old.

Alice knows that she was fortunate to be adopted when she was 12 years of age. Most children that age would be considered "unadoptable." When she arrived at the home of her new parents, Mr. and Mrs. W. J. Hunter, she learned she had a new brother, too. Robert Hunter was adopted as a baby and at the time of Alice's adoption he was eight years old. Robert and Alice continue to be "family."

As the following story states, it was Betty's desire to keep the siblings in touch with each other. She succeeded with this. Since their 1992 reunion, some of the sisters went to visit their only brother, Raymond in South Carolina where he resides in a Veteran's Hospital.

More recently, three have passed away. Halo in 1995 at Salem, Oregon; Arlene in 2002 at Princeton, Minnesota; and Betty on July 25th, 2003 at Phoenix, Arizona. The siblings will always be indebted to Betty for keeping the link connected between them.

The Home We Shared

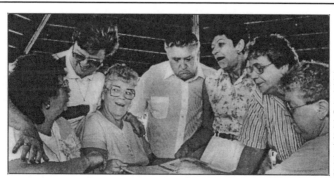

Left to Right – Evelyn Beall, Alice Tannehill, Gloria Wang, Raymond Seccombe, Halo West, Arlene Benik, and Betty Shull

Siblings Reunited after 48 Years

By Lucia Marinaccio, Staff Writer
From "The Fargo Forum" – August 2, 1992

At a glance, the Hyelden family reunion looks like a typical family gathering.

Comparing their day-to-day lives, the six sisters and one brother marvel at how similar they all are.

"We even make potato salad the same way," one of the sisters says with a laugh. It must be in the genes.

The siblings, ranging in age from 53 to 64, all speak at once in a jumble of accents, reminiscing about their early years in North Dakota.

They all share candid personalities, the same dark eyes and a handful of childhood memories. The few childhood memories they exchange are priceless; they are the only memories they have of each other. In 1944 Halo, Gloria, Alice, Betty, Arlene, Raymond and Evelyn were taken to the North Dakota Children's Home in Fargo after their mother died giving birth to Evelyn. One by one the children left the home to start life with a new family. They were told to forget the old, but they didn't.

Saturday, 48 years later, the seven were reunited for the first time at Trollwood Park in Fargo.

"It's like we've never been apart," Evelyn says. "I cried for years every night because I wanted my sisters, and now we're a family again."

As the family sat around a table talking, tears of joy and pain started and stopped and started again, triggered by happy memories of being together as children, or painful memories of being separated.

"Some of us were adopted into homes that gave us love and attention, but some weren't so fortunate," Alice said.

Evelyn and Raymond, the two youngest, went to live with a couple from Langdon, ND.

A family that lived in Bismarck, ND adopted Alice. There, she grew up and later met her husband. Arlene's new family lived in De-Lamere, ND.

"I remember Arlene was the first to leave the Home," Alice says. "She just disappeared one Sunday and didn't come back."

Gloria remained at the Children's Home for many years, taking care of the small children. Eventually, she opened up her own daycare center.

Halo was the only child who never stayed at the Children's Home. She was the oldest, and at age 15 she was taken to Grand Forks, ND, by her social worker. "I went to Grand Forks, worked and from then on I was a forgotten person," she says.

A family in Hope, ND adopted Betty. It was with their encouragement that she initiated the seemingly impossible task of reuniting the family.

Few of the siblings were able to gain contact through the years, so Betty relentlessly pressured the social workers to release the whereabouts of her sisters and brother.

"If Betty would have given up, we wouldn't be here today." Alice says.

But today the family refuses to focus on the past. "We can't change the past, all we can change is the future," Halo says.

"Now, I know I have family I can visit. It's a wonderful feeling." Alice says.

Soon she will return to her home in Ohio, Halo to Oregon, Betty to Arizona, Arlene to Minnesota, Evelyn to Washington, Raymond to South Carolina and Gloria to her home in Fargo, with the promise that they won't let another 48 years pass before getting together again.

The Home We Shared

Meta Mae Madden, Where Are You?

Before I could finish this section of stories by "children," who are now adults, I have to write a few words about one special child. This child would now be over 70 years old.

As I made my contacts with the people who have shared their stories, most asked, "Where is Meta Mae Madden?" I, too, wondered, as I have many photos of her. She was a favorite friend of all of us.

Meta came to the Home as a small child. Miss Jean Love wrote a letter to Mr. Bridgiford at the Children's Village in 1978 giving information about a set of photos from the Home. Jean related this information:

"Meta came to the Receiving Home with a brother a few years older. Her mother had died, possibly of Tuberculosis. Her brother was placed for adoption. Meta lived at the Home and was under our care for several years between stays at the TB Sanitarium at Dunseith. She was always a "poor eater," so I never required her to eat more than she wanted.

Meta Mae Madden about four years old.
Photo by Florence Wiest.

Once when I was traveling with her to or from Dunseith, we were in the train diner. When I ordered only milk for her and a full meal for myself, a man sitting at the opposite table was distressed because this pathetic child was not having more to eat. He apparently couldn't accept my reason comfortably and in mid-morning came and asked if we would be his guests for lunch. I accepted his invitation.

Years after, he spoke to me in the lobby of a Jamestown hotel, asking whether I wasn't the worker he had seen on the train with the little crippled girl. He had never been able to get her out of his mind. I told him of her progress, which pleased him very much.

When Meta was in her teens, I was working in Omaha and received a request from the North Dakota Children's Home to meet Meta at the train, keep her overnight, and put her on the train for Los Angeles, where her father would meet her, in the a.m."

In honor of Meta, both Florence Wiest and I have shared our photos taken of her. Since she lived at the Home over a number of years, many

Meta Mae Madden about 10 years old.
Photo by Florence Wiest.

other children grew to enjoy her kind and loving personality. Meta is one of the children remembered with great fondness both by children and staff.

Meta and the other children, who shared their stories in this section of my book, are just a few of the children who lived at the Home. From 1900 to 1957, there were 9,000 children who stayed one or more years with the caring staff at "The Home We Shared."

Meta Mae and Dorothy — the knitted dress that kept growing as Dorothy grew.

A Walking Tour
Through the North Dakota Children's Home

The Home We Shared

Approaching the Home, you walked up a 12-foot wide sidewalk towards the front door. First, you walked up a set of cement steps, then, a set of wooden steps to the front porch. The full-length front porch had a rail held up by wooden spindles. There were tall wooden posts holding up the second floor porch. Both porches extended the full length of the Home. At the south end of the first floor porch was a set of wooden steps. The second floor porch ended in metal steps for a fire escape. All led to the playground area.

The Office Staff used the front door to meet birth parents, children, and adopting parents. It was "off limits" to the rest of the staff and children living there. When one entered through the front door, you came into a six-foot vestibule that opened into a large open foyer. There, you could see a five-foot wide circular staircase leading to the second floor. These stairs, too, were "off limits" to the residing children, but possibly used by the staff for hurried travel between floors.

All of the first floor rooms had twelve-foot ceilings. Immediately, you had a sense of the immenseness of the home. To the left was the Library. It had four windows, all six feet in height. These windows let in the sunlight from the west and the north. Below each window were built-in bookshelves that could be used for sitting on, looking out the windows, or for reading. Between the windows were many more bookshelves lined with books.

On the east wall, there was a davenport, chairs, and lamp. There were some easy chairs, as well. For children's study times and research, there were a couple of student library tables and chairs.

Postcard photo, taken after 1912.
The "Receiving Home" cottage was moved from
10th Street to the back of the Home and faced 8th Avenue.
Then, an addition was added to the south end of the original 1900 Home.

From the photo collection of florence Wiest Faust.

The Home We Shared

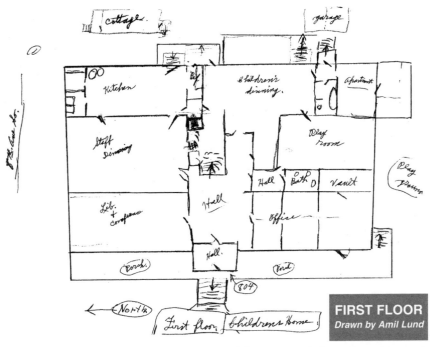

FIRST FLOOR
Drawn by Amil Lund

During the day, the library was used by the social workers to meet with families and show future adopting parents their new child or children. Again, during office hours this area was "off limits." But, in the evening and on weekends, children visited the library to check out books, read, and study in this area. Along with the large supply of books were children's magazines and encyclopedias.

Towards the south and opposite the library was the office area. This space was divided into a reception room and two other office spaces. A large walk-in vault was located on the east wall for the safe keeping of records on each child, financial statements, information on adoptions or foster care.

From the foyer, there were two sets of French doors with curtains over the windows on the backsides. The ones to the right led to a set of closets, children's restroom, and the playroom. The French doors to the left, opened into the large Staff Dining Room. There, two six-foot windows brought light in from the north. One-half of this room was used for a sitting room. Directly in front of the north wall was the long, dining table that could easily seat ten of the workers. It was always set formally with tablecloths and Jewel Tea dishes. Each staff person was supplied with a special shaped silver napkin holder — some had their initials engraved on their holder — thus, the linen napkins were used for a few days before being laundered.

The Home We Shared

Some younger children in the Children's Dining Room.

Beside the west wall was the Kimball piano. Towards the south side was davenport with a sofa table behind it that had a lamp and the daily papers on it. This sitting area was at least five feet from the south wall, allowing for the constant stream of persons passing to get to the backstairs that led to the second floor. This was the only way the children could reach their bedrooms.

On the east wall was a large buffet that held the complete set of Jewell Tea dishes. The "buffet style" staff dinners were served from here, as each person arrived at different times because of their assigned chores. Six feet either side of the buffet was two doors.

The door on the south led into the Kitchen. The other north door went directly into the Dishwashing Room. This room contained two large sinks and many cupboards for dish storage. Usually, the teenage girls took their turns at these sinks to wash, drain, wipe and put away the dishes after each meal.

Directly to the south of this room was the Kitchen. In the center was the workspace, a large six by 12-foot butcher-block table. Under it were shelves for large kettles, pots, and pans. Also, there were drawers for the cooking utensils. The huge, black, Monarch gas stove took all the space on the west wall. The north wall had a kitchen sink and in the northeast corner sat a "potato peeler." This machine looked much like a small, front-opening wash machine. Potatoes would be dumped into it, the door closed, and the machine turned on. This circulated and bumped the potatoes against the abrasive sides. Water ran over them, too, taking the peels away to a drain. When it was stopped, the peels were gone.

Next to the peeler, stood the bakery style mixer. Many cakes, cookies, and loaves of bread were produced from that machine. Two large windows to the east let in the morning sunlight. North of the peeler, was a

The Home We Shared

Television viewing in the evenings in the alcove of the Children's Dining Room. At left is the playroom entrance with picket fence gate, 1952.

large pantry with cupboards to the ceiling. Large bins for flour and other bulk staples were in the lower level cupboards.

At the south end of the kitchen, an outside entry was separated from the Kitchen by a wall. In that location was a built-in, four-door refrigerator with large, heavy handles for openers. These were often found in the '30s grocery stores. A place to hang your coat and cleaning materials was, also, beside the back door.

A south hallway led from the Kitchen. Immediately to the right, a stairway led to the basement. Continuing walking straight ahead, you came to the Children's Dining Room. On your left was a built in buffet; often displaying a huge flower arrangement donated after memorial services.

Above the buffet, high cupboards rising to the ceiling contained "Fiesta" dishes, enough to serve 60 children on special holidays. A place setting consisted of large plates, sauce dishes, pie plates, and tumblers, all in beautiful colors. Another low, side cupboard held the daily used items, such as the everyday dishes, salt, pepper, creamers and sugar bowls.

On the east wall, next to the cupboards was another back door that matched the one in the Kitchen. This opened onto the same 15-foot porch. This dining room door was the most frequented door, as the chil-

The Home We Shared

"Let's line up big to little in our playroom," 1948.

dren moved through it to and from school and playground.

Inside, directly opposite the east outside door, a small vestibule and closet were located under the circular front stairway. Here the brooms, dustpans, dust mops, and shoeshine kits were stored.

Back in the dining room you would find a low table and row of highchairs for the small children. Along the walls were eight high tables for the older children. At each table were four wooden "ice-cream parlor" chairs. These tables not only provided space where their meals were eaten; but also, a place to play games, make puzzles, color in books, write, and cut out paper dolls. In 1952, a small TV was mounted in the corner of the dining room; thus, TV watching was added to the children's activities.

A door to the south led into the Lund's apartment. The apartment consisted of one large room and bath until 1945 when an additional room was added, and an outside entrance when the porch was added.

On the west wall, a hinged picket fence gate opened to the Playroom. This is where the preschool children spent their days at play and afternoon naps. When home from school, older children would assist with leading games. A portable, wooden slide was usually in the center. The west wall had a closet full of play items and mats. The south wall had two large windows and a door facing the playground. This was the shortest way to the outdoors. A nearby closet held coats and jackets for the cooler weather.

A large restroom was located nearby on the northwest corner of the playroom. This contained a row of very small flush toilets and two low sinks for the toddlers. There was one regular size toilet and sink, as well.

The Home We Shared

Going back to the Staff Dining Room and up the stairs, you reached the second floor. At the top of the stairs, the large community bathroom was located. It was the place that the children were brought for their first baths upon arrival. Along the right wall were cupboards and a long bench with lift up covers all used for clothes storage.

Kids in the playroom.

There was only one old fashioned toilet in this bathroom with a water closet high up on the wall. For flushing you pulled down on the wooden handle hanging on a chain from the water chamber above. Next, there was a long, trough sink, with at least two sets of water faucets, so a few children at a time could wash their hands or brush their teeth. Set back into an alcove was the large, raised bathtub with the steps leading up to it. A dressing table was attached, so younger children could be dried and dressed more easily.

Returning to the hall, turning right, and walking down a short hall, there was a restroom to one side, a Sewing/Mending room at the end. The opposite wall contained a closet with cleaning supplies and a door that opened to steps leading to an attic, which topped the whole house and was used for storage.

Now, back to the second floor stairs and walking directly west, there were more closets. The first room on the right was the Teenage Girls' Room. It was a large room with many twin beds and a few bunk beds lining one wall. They had their own private bathroom and walk-in closet.

Just around the corner, there were two Little Girls' Dormitories. One was directly over the Library, the other over the offices. Sandwiched in-between these two rooms was a small apartment, where Miss Esther Hartvikson, the head nurse for the babies and toddlers resided. I assume she had her own bathroom, but I never visited that area. Sometimes, she left her door open and one could see the large curtained windows facing towards the upstairs porch.

All of the upstairs rooms on the south, west and north had the six-foot windows, allowing ample light into the rooms or opened for fresh air. One inner room just outside the nurseries and boys' bedroom had a dumb waiter in it for bringing clean clothes back up to the second floor. It contained twin beds for the older boys.

Directly over the Children's Dining Room was a large Boy's Dormitory. It had smaller windows in a row that allowed for good lighting, too. Three

The Home We Shared

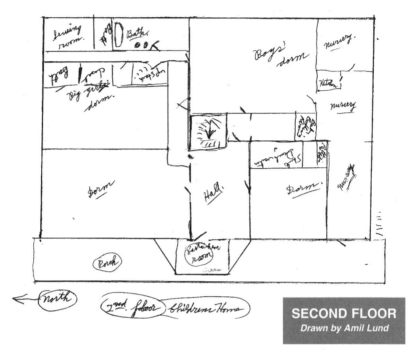

SECOND FLOOR
Drawn by Amil Lund

walls of this room were lined with bunk beds made of heavy lumber. The bunk creators were Mr. Harold Bond and Amil Lund. On the east wall under the windows were built-in wardrobes for their hanging clothes and shelves for storage. In the '40s, a long, round, tube-shaped fire escape was placed on the east wall. The children were instructed to slide down it, if there were a fire.

Walking from that room to the south, was an enclosed Doctor's Examining Room. It had an examining table, glassed-in shelf areas for instruments, baby scale, and sink. The next room was the Newborn Nursery where the three-day to two-month-old infants stayed. The metal cribs lined the two outside, windowed walls.

To the west of this room was the Toddler Nursery for youngsters two-months to two years of age. A small kitchen was walled off in one corner. The larger room held many cribs, highchairs, strollers, and jump chairs. There were boxes of toys to play with in a large central area.

The clothes, potty training area, tubs, and dressing table were in the next two areas. The main room had just the lower half of Dutch doors on the kitchen and dressing room. Thus, the young ones crawling or walking could not leave the area.

Under the house was a full basement with cement floor. The section below the Library and half of the Staff Dining Room held the new clothes and toys for Christmas and Birthday gifts. There were tall wardrobes for

The Home We Shared

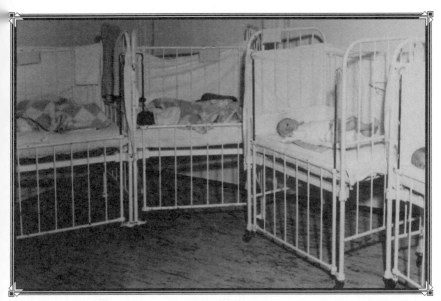

Newborn nursery.

Bunk beds in boys' dormitory, built by Mr. Bond and Mr. Lund.

The Home We Shared

Myra and the two Dorothy's, Christmas, 1946.

the clothes, many shelves for toys, large tables where the sorting and wrapping took place.

Each day, over a period of eight to 10 hours, the efficient Laundry produced volumes of clean clothes. It was located below the east half of the Staff Dining Room and Kitchen. It was "old fashioned" to the laundries of today, but advanced and adequate for this family of 50 to 75 children. Until the late '40s, all washing was done in a wringer type electric machine. All of the clothes were pushed through the wringer from the washing machine to the other two tubs to be rinsed. In the late '40s, two large front loading washers were added. But nonetheless, the original machine continued to be used, too.

Next, clothes were placed in an extractor that whirled the wet clothes until most of the moisture was gone. From there, they were placed in a monster of a gas heated drier. The rows of flames could be seen below the metal clothesbasket, which was six feet long, and three feet in diameter. After the lid was closed, a lever was released to send the basket on its circling motion. When the clothes were dried, a worker stopped the motion and began to pull out the clothes. Usually, a handle of a broomstick was used to pull the hot clothes from this hot machine. Sometimes wet clothes were carried past the garage to clothes lines that paralleled the alley.

Some large items, such as sheets, went through the mangle. Its length was four feet with a round device that looked like a giant curling iron. The wrinkled materials were pushed under the hot roller and came out over the top, flattened.

Dresses and shirts were ironed at the ironing board in the center of the room. These were the days when there was no polyester mixed in with the cotton. With at least 25 girls in the home at a time, there were

The Home We Shared

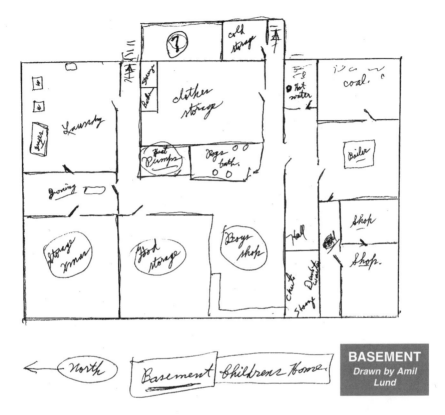

BASEMENT
Drawn by Amil Lund

many starched dresses to be ironed. Water from a sprinkle bottle moistened the material just enough to allow for ironing.

All of the soiled clothes from the nurseries were sent down to the basement through a clothes chute in the potty room and returned by the dumb waiter. Both of these "time savers" were at the opposite end of the basement near the Furnace Room. Diapers and infant clothing had to be washed daily. They were carried from the chute to the laundry.

East of the Laundry, there was a double door that opened inward and revealed a set of stairs. Above the stairs you pushed upward to open the cellar doors. This was the pathway for the laundresses to carry baskets of wet clothing to the lines, which were 75 feet away. Regardless of the distance, the clothes were hung whenever the weather permitted. Near these doors, a small room held the barrels of washing supplies, next, a half bathroom.

A short walk down a hall to the west brought you to the large, locked, food storage room. The 25- by 25-foot space had four wooden shelves all around the room. Industrial-sized cans of food were set on the shelves in neat rows. In the center, were fresh foods kept on pallets, barrels of dried food, and boxes of paper products.

Moving past the storage area you came into a room sectioned off into many areas. It was mainly the Boys' Project Area. One section was a screened room built around an oversized water heater. Another part had a large coatroom with wooden pegs on the walls for the boys' outdoor clothing. A wooden wall elevated a foot from the cement floor surrounded the boys' lavatory. It had a wooden swinging door on it with a big spring, and would bang loudly as the boys when in and out of the area. The boys were encouraged to use the door and not crawl under the wooden wall.

The boys' work area was located below the front foyer of the house. It had a long workbench and tools for the boys' projects. There were wooden shelves to one side with cubbyholes to hold their possessions. Comic books, puzzles, coloring books, airplanes, and trucks could be kept in their box. The older boys created model airplanes from thin balsam wood and tissue paper.

Another area was used for storing the windows and screens during the off seasons. This is where the clothes chute and dumb waiter were located, also.

The furnace room and coal bin were to the south of the boys' area, Amil's workbench and tools were in a separate locked area. Behind that room, he had built the small dining room and kitchen where the Lund family could have a private meal at least two to four times a month. Here

Playground, 1940s.

The Home We Shared

Dorothy and Myra enjoying the playground, 1952.

the Lunds' could have their friends in for a meal prepared by Mary. Also, Amil had his darkroom for developing photos and all of his equipment for his photography hobby.

Going back out to the furnace room and turning to the right, you traveled along a long cement hallway with a large storage room on the left. Here used clothing or off-season clothing items were sorted. Shoes, overshoes, underwear, and baby clothes were on shelves in boxes. Next to it, was a dark damp fruit and vegetable cellar.

Continuing to the east, you came to a stairway leading to the outdoors. This was the entrance the boys were to use as they traveled in and out to the playground, restrooms, and project area.

There is one mystery area, located opposite the above mentioned food cellar. A space with a door to the outside, that neither my father nor I could recall going into. A padlock hung on the outside door that faced the north. I have decided it was another food cellar that only the cook used.

The backyard had a double garage and play equipment. Swings, teeter totters, merry-go-round; all made from metal like school playgrounds displayed in the '30s. A 12-foot sandbox with many sand toys was located near the swings.

Near the alley, the 30-foot clotheslines were strung between three sets of poles. Next to the clotheslines and along the alley, the two burn-barrels sat. Hopefully, these were not used at the time the clothes were hung on the lines.

Behind the Home and facing north was an average sized, two-story house. This was used to isolate children with contagious diseases, living quarters for a few of the single workers, and a home where the Lund family lived for six years, 1951-1957.

Mr. Harold Bond and family lived across the alley, directly behind the Home. During Mr. Bond's times off from work, a knock on his door brought him to the Home for consultation. He was ready to resolve any problem.

This completes the walking tour of our special Home.

The Home We Shared

George W. Jenson, Treasurer of the North Dakota Children's Home Society Board for 40 years, and Amil J. Lund (my dad), Engineer and Housefather for the Home for 33 years, were honored at a banquet on Thursday, November 14, 1963, at Oak Manor in Fargo, North Dakota. I was living in Illinois and teaching at a high school as sole breadwinner for our family of four putting my first husband through seminary. Thus, I could not attend.

As I look at my dad's speech notes, I wonder if I might have typed them up for him, as the papers look like they came from our family typewriter. He had underlined certain things to be emphasized. He continued to work for The Children's Village another 20 years. He retired in 1984.

Remarks by Mr. Lund, November 14, 1963

I would like to acknowledge your act of honoring Mr. Jenson and myself tonight, and to thank you on behalf of Mary; my parents, Oscar and Betsy Lund; my brother, Millard and wife; and daughter, Myra, for your kind invitation.

There are many things we could recall, out of what we call the "good old days of the Home." In 1930, there was very little that was good about the economy of the state and the ability of the citizens to support good charitable agencies.

It was at this time that Mr. Bond, Superintendent of the Home, wanted me to help him, so in November of 1930, I joined the staff of the Children's Home.

We were facing the Depression that had begun with the crash of the stock market and the state was also heading into a serious drought.

During this period, the agency had a great number of children, arising out of the Depression and drought. The only thing that saved us was the fact that a dollar went a long way, that food was cheap, and that the government, in one way or another, tried to meet some of the emergencies.

It may be of interest to you, that during Mr. Jenson's and my time at the agency, the Home was deeply involved in a Crippled Children's Program.

This came about in this way. The Federal Social Security Act had made sums available and the state received $29,000, for the purpose of taking a census of the crippled children of the state and treating as many as possible.

Announcement of this was made in 1937, with the state contributing $22,000. The Elk's organization took the census, since it has a long history of services to crippled children.

It was agreed that Fargo would take the bulk of the patients, although some other town with hospitals took some of the children. Dr. H.J. Fortin and Dr. J.C. Swanson were in charge of the surgical treatment.

In order to have a receiving center and a convalescent home for the children, Mr. Harold Bond, then the superintendent, agreed to move the

The Home We Shared

children out of the 10th Street Home to the Detroit Lakes area for the summer.

Cottages on Lake Melissa and Little Floyd Lakes were rented, for the summer months, while the Crippled Children were using the Home.

The census taken by the Elk's revealed about 1,500 children were in need of some kind of treatment. Some had infantile paralysis, others had deformities such as: club feet, birth injuries, congenital hips, malformed spine or neck cords, etc.

A total of 200 patients were accepted for the first summer and the Society handled about 104 children for the program. Mrs. Lund (then, Mary Leazer) took children to Floyd Lake. We selected the children who had whooping cough at the time, to go to Floyd. The children who were well, we took to Melissa. I believe Mrs. Raines had the Lake Melissa group. Mr. Bond and I helped at the Fargo end.

We had to meet trains, take the children to the Home, take them to the clinics for their appointments, then to the hospital, then to the Home, and finally back on the trains. You can imagine that this was hard work, since many of these children could not walk and many had heavy casts or braces.

On weekends, I had to deliver supplies to the lakes and to keep those projects going for our own children under the care of our agency.

The county welfare boards in the state handled details out in the local areas, getting consent from the parents. Miss Theodora Allen, the head of the children's bureau of the state welfare board, was in general charge of the program.

In 1939, Camp Watson, on Lake Pelican was given to the agency. This cottage had stood empty for several years, when the family stopped using it. A few years before, the Episcopal Church had rented its Holiday House to the Children's Home. It was two lots away from Camp Watson.

When the estate sold its possessions and the camp was given to us, it was in poor shape. The weeds were high and the buildings needed repair.

My wife, Mary, and I worked hard during the next few summers to get the place in shape. The Crippled Children's Program continued each year for about ten years, but we were able to keep the Home children in one spot at Camp Watson, because of its large size.

As Mr. Jenson suggested, many of our problems in those days are the same ones we face today.

I heard Mr. Bond speak of the anxiety of the public welfare agencies to take over the functions of the private child welfare agencies; of the shortages of funds to do a good job and of the shortages of trained manpower everywhere in welfare.

Mr. Bond often said that the agency had done well and has many friends. One reason for this, he said, was that we have always responded to calls for help. Welfare Boards and Juvenile Commissioners, he said,

The Home We Shared

soon came to know this and appreciate it. He also believed that the agency had friends because it always responded promptly to communications; always acknowledged gifts and courtesies; and never turned down a job it felt it could accomplish.

Mr. Bond also believed that a great majority of the children under our care, turned out very well as adults.

The old Home on 10th street was never satisfactory and was the cause of much worry on the part of Mr. Bond, Mr. Olslund, and myself. It was a fire hazard, hard to maintain and overcrowded. The nursery for babies was never considered to be really satisfactory.

The three new cottages of The Children's Village on South University Drive, while larger and more of a responsibility, are much more satisfactory all around. This is quite a change from the old home, but the same problems continue to handicap the children we have now. There is little change in the social problems.

My wife, Mary, joined the Children's Home Staff in 1926. She worked as "Matron" as it was called at that time until we shifted to the new agency quarters.

At the Home, Matron meant house mother, nurse, cook, and summer camp operator. While my job was co-camp operator, chauffeur, and general all-around handyman. But we have enjoyed these years and all the hundreds of children and we look forward to more of the same.

I want to thank all of you!"

**Amil and Steve Hohnadel at the time of Amil's retirement.
Amil turned his responsiblities over to Steve.**

ACKNOWLEDGEMENTS

The Home We Shared

For The Home We Shared History: To each of you, a "Thank you" for your assistance.

The Village Family Service Center of Fargo, North Dakota:
 Gary Wolsky, President, for sharing the Home's historical information and **Tammy Noteboom,** Director of Communications, for editing this book many times, and **Laurie Neill** for the cover design and book layout.

The North Dakota State University Institute of Regional Studies, Fargo, North Dakota:
 John E. Bye, John Hallberg, and Tom Riley for sharing their "Home Finder" file, Florence Crittenton Home file, and photos.

State Historical Society of North Dakota Heritage Center, Bismarck, North Dakota:
 Delores Vyzralek, Chief Librarian for researching Home information.
 Sharon Silengo, Photo Archivist for Heritage Center.

Special Friends:
 Bill Snyder of Fargo, formerly with WDAY, movie producer, and historian. He helped me with the names of buildings and families.
 Howard Ralston, formerly of Petersburg, North Dakota, and presently of Rochester, Minnesota, for his illustrations for "Burke's Journeys" story of Andrew Burke.
 Susan Morris who assisted with sorting historical items and found information on the Internet concerning "Daddy Hall."
 Jan Hanson of Fargo for sharing her grandmother's story and introducing me to the darling child, "Topsey."
 Jennifer Radack's for her stories about Mabel Miller and Gloria Wang.
 Robert C. Olslund for sharing his memories of the Home's last years.

Children's Stories: A special "Thank you" for sharing your stories to:
 Robert and Delores Barringer for Hazel's Story
 May Berge Bredeson   Dorothy Noell Anderson
 Margaret Wogh   Delbert Knowlen
 Florence Wiest Faust   Alice Tannehill
 Alton Graf   Gloria Wang
 Rosalie Reis Rosenaw
 Royal Wayne Bahr

Albert Nelson, my husband, who has been supportive through the long hours it took to produce and publish, "The Home We Shared."

The Home We Shared

About the Author

Dorothy Alberna Lund Nelson was born at Fargo, North Dakota, and raised in the North Dakota Children's Home. She and her parents, Mary (Leazer) and Amil Lund, shared a one-room apartment at the rear of the facility. Later, another room was added, when her parents adopted her sister, Myra.

Dorothy earned her Bachelor of Science Degree from North Dakota State University, Fargo. She taught school and led recreation at centers in North Dakota, South Dakota, Illinois and Minnesota for 17 years. At that time she was married and raised a family that consisted of her three sons, foster children, and Myra's children. Twenty of those years were spent in parsonages as a pastor's wife.

After taking some classes on the Master's level at Mankato State University, Mankato, Minnesota, Dorothy completed and passed an exam to become a Certified Therapeutic Recreation Specialist and was one of the first in the USA to be a Certified Activities Consultant. From 1972 to 1995, she was the Activities Director and Volunteer Coordinator at Long-Term Health Care Facilities in five different communities.

Dorothy is proud of her sons, who are in "serving" occupations. Norm Barnhart and his wife, Mia, are Professional Magicians. Each are concerned that children have good entertainment. They have a daughter, Jasmine.

Scott Barnhart and his wife, Sharon, are both Registered Nurses. Scott spends weekends with patients in a hospital Intensive Care Unit, while Sharon is involved in Cardiac Research and graduate school. They have two daughters, Sarah and Nicole.

Weston Barnhart Lund has taught "English Second Language" in many places: Morocco as a Peace Corps Volunteer, inner-city schools of New York City, and Japanese High Schools. He speaks five languages. Music is always a part of his classroom activities.

Dorothy lives in Rochester, Minnesota, with her husband, Albert Nelson. They enjoy meeting relatives, genealogy, traveling, and music. He assists her in driving to various communities and carrying props for her presentations.

She is pleased that she has created this book of history about a most important place for children in years past.

Also by Dorothy Lund Nelson
"The Dahl Family Album"
Co-author, Almira Dahl

"Burke's Journeys"
Illustrated by Howard Ralston